Dr. Yirmi Goldin's
HASHEM'S MAGNIFICENT MACHINES

How "New" Ideas MERELY COPY THE CREATOR

The Torah Vet Series

DISTRIBUTED BY FELDHEIM

ISBN 978-1-68025-380-1

Copyright © 2019 by Yirmi Goldin
yirmigoldin@gmail.com

All rights reserved. No part of this publication may be translated, reproduced, stored in a retrieval system or transmitted, in any form or by any means, electronic, mechanical, photocopying, recording or otherwise, without prior permission in writing from the publishers.

Distributed by:	Distributed in Europe by:	Distributed in Australia by:
Feldheim Publishers	Lehmanns	Golds World of Judaica
POB 43163 / Jerusalem, Israel	+44-0-191-430-0333	+613 95278775
208 Airport Executive Park	info@lehmanns.co.uk	info@golds.com.au
Nanuet, NY 10954	www.lehmanns.co.uk	www.golds.com.au
www.feldheim.com		

Printed in China

10 9 8 7 6 5 4 3 2 1

Caricatures: Matt Golding

Cover: Michael Silverstein

I wish to express my infinite thanks to:

- my wife Janine, for her patience, encouragement and support.
- my children Devorah and Yudi Landau, Gavriella, Tuvia and Shira, for their "kids' perspective."
- my parents Mordechai and Basya — perfect role models in every way.
- the staff and *avreichim* of Kollel Beth HaTalmud (the Lakewood Kollel in Melbourne), most especially Rosh HaKollel HaRav Binyomin Wurzburger *shlita*, for his ongoing guidance.
- R' Doniel Lanzer, for his incredible support.
- renowned author and teacher Rabbi Yisroel Greenwald, who constantly pushes and encourages me to share my enthusiasm for Hashem's creations with anyone who will listen.
- friends Brad and Mandy Dembo, my first teachers.
- Rabbi David Kahn, for his expert editing.
- Manfred Cohen, for his visionary layout of the first volume, and Michael Silverstein, for building on that framework to beautifully design the volume in your hands.
- HaRav HaGaon Rabbi Avigdor Miller *zt"l*, whose writings, *shiurim* and *hashkafos* affect me every day.

I end these acknowledgments with the following gratitude and *tefillah*: Each member of mankind is absolutely indebted to You, Hashem, for the bounty of gifts You shower us with. May it be Your will that the reader of these pages finds connection and closeness to You, and the desire to serve You meaningfully.

CONTENTS

Dear Kids
7

Guns / PISTOL SHRIMP **8-11**

Rockets / BOMBARDIER BEETLE **12-17**

GPS / MONARCH BUTTERFLY.................................... **18-21**

Taser / ELECTRIC EEL.. **22-25**

Camouflage / MIMIC OCTOPUS **26-31**
(Snake Caterpillar, Fork-Tailed Drongo,
Leaf Fish, Ant Spider, Stonefish, Owl Butterfly)

Antifreeze / WOOD FROG **32-39**
(HASHEM'S INCREDIBLE FROGS: Flying Frog,
Skin Blister Frog, Turtle Frog, Poison Dart Frog, Cocoon
Frog, Baby Swallowing Frog, Glass Frog)

Sports Cars / CHEETAH **40-47**
(HASHEM'S FASTEST & SLOWEST ANIMALS:
Peregrine Falcon, South Californian Mite, Black Marlin,
Three-Toed Sloth, Banana Slug, Lichens)

Welding Helmets / CHAMELEON..................... **48-55**
(Cuttlefish, Golden Tortoise Beetle)

Sunscreen / HIPPOPOTAMUS................................. **56-59**

Thermal Imaging / VIPER SNAKE **60-65**
(Mantis Shrimp, "All-Eye" Brittle Star)

Jet Engine Cones / PEREGRINE FALCON **66-69**

All-Weather Clothing
/ POLAR BEAR, SEA OTTER.. **70-73**

Autonomous Cars / LOCUSTS............................ **74-79**
(Pebble Toad, Pangolin, Flying Fish, Pom-Pom Crab)

Composites / BEES **80-87**
(Malleefowl, Paper Wasp, Redback Spider,
Edible-Nest Swiftlet)

Photo Credits
89

APPROBATIONS

בס"ד

22 SHIMON HATZADIK STREET / JERUSALEM 91180 ISRAEL / TEL: 972-2-581-0315

As the earth spins on its tilted axis and progresses along its elliptical tour of duty around the sun, it turns its cheek towards the glowing ball from a different vantage point every day. Thus, each day is of a slightly different duration from the preceding one, no two days exactly the same in length.

This is not a coincidence, but a reminder of the distinctiveness inherent in each day. Today is not a duplicate of yesterday, nor will it be repeated tomorrow. Each day is separate and unique. No second can be recaptured once it has passed, nor can it ever be repeated.

There are ways, however, that moments can be preserved, perpetuated and extended into eternity. Should a man utilize his time for mitzvos and live by the dictates of His infinite wisdom — then he succeeds in directing time and energy towards a Divine purpose, and unlocks the secret of eternity.

It gives me great pleasure to see the intriguing book, *Hashem's Magnificent Machines*, by Dr. Yirmi Goldin. I am confident that this work will inspire many with a deeper understanding of Hashem's creations and thus raise the consciousness of Hashem in our lives, and assist us to live a meaningful life governed by Torah and mitzvah observance.

There are many similarities between a painter and a writer. One works with his brush, the other with his pen. One sketches with the richness of his colors, the other with the richness of his language. Each attempts to portray an image of his model, one through the eyes of the flesh and the other through the eyes of the spirit. Dr. Yirmi Goldin has succeeded with this masterpiece to sketch with both his brush and pen.

May Hashem Yisborach grant the author long life and health to continue to merit the community with further Torah works.

With Torah blessings,
Rabbi Yonason Wiener

בס"ד

שמואל קמנצקי
Rabbi S. Kamenetsky

2018 Upland Way
Philadelphia, PA 19131

Home: 215-473-2798
Study: 215-473-1212

Dear Dr. Goldin, נ"י

I have seen your books and found them to be both informative and entertaining. I am happy to hear that you are now publishing the second volume. It is clear from the content expressed in your writing that you have broad knowledge and that the clear presentation of ideas will engage children's interest. Adults, too, will find insight in the depth of its content. It is my hope that your books will be of benefit to many, since learning about the נפלאות הבורא is a means of strengthening *emunah* in HaKadosh Baruch Hu in the next generation.

You have managed to crystalize and elucidate the connection between modern inventions and the intricate details that comprise HaKadosh Baruch Hu's בריאה, inspiring the reader to marvel at מה רבו מעשיך ה'.

I would like to give you a *berachah*: just as your previous book has been successful in inspiring young and old alike, may you continue to go מחיל אל חיל in your לימוד והרבצת התורה for many days.

S. Kamenetsky

KOLLEL BETH HATALMUD
YEHUDA FISHMAN INSTITUTE

כולל בית התלמוד
זכרון יהודה פישמאן

Herzog Community Centre ❖ Yaakov and Clara Lanzer Advanced Learning Program ❖ Rabbi Joseph and Stera Gutnick Study Hall ❖ Rodney and Lynda Adler Tape Library ❖ Yocheved Kaila a"h Bas R' Binyomin Zev Wurzburger Women's Program ❖ Tova Herszberg a"h Youth Foundation ❖ PLP University Program

Rabbi B Z Wurzburger Rosh HaKollel
Rabbi E Saftlas Menahel
Dr D Lanzer President
T (03) 9527 6156
F (03) 9527 8034

בס"ד

סידרי הכולל לכבוד יעקב וחיה לנצר
362a Carlisle St, Balaclava
Victoria 3183 Australia
@ office@kollel.com.au
W www.kollel.com.au

Cheshvan 5779, October 2018

My dear friend, Dr. Goldin, has presented me with another beautiful manuscript, the follow-up to his first book, *Hashem Invented Skyscrapers*, which has received much praise and, *baruch Hashem*, has been very successful. I therefore extend the same *divrei berachah* as before:

The follow-up book, *Hashem's Magnificent Machines*, demonstrates many aspects of *gadlus HaBorei*. This *sefer*, too, has inspired me greatly.

The author has achieved phenomenal heights in his *avodas Hashem*, which were instrumental in producing this exceptional work.

This book gives us the ability to fulfill the directives of the *Chovos HaLevavos* in *Shaar HaBechinah*. Seeing and understanding the greatness of Hashem in the physical realm allows us to appreciate our Creator even more, and fulfill His Torah and mitzvos with greater enthusiasm.

May it be the Creator's will that the desired effect of this book should be achieved *lehagdil Torah uleha'adirah*. May Hashem grant the author to go *me'chayil el chayil* — to achieve tremendous success in all his endeavors, together with his *chosheve* family.

Rabbi Wurzburger

Rosh HaKollel

The Wiener Edition

Dedicated in loving memory of
Dr. Saul Wiener
שאול בן הרב יוסף וינר זצ"ל
*by his wife Fay, his children,
grandchildren and great grandchildren.*

Dr. Wiener was a proud Orthodox Jew and a pioneering scientist and physician. The study of Torah was primary and absolutely central to his life, as was his deep appreciation of the wonders of Hashem's world which surrounded him. He studied in the yeshiva of Rav Breuer in Frankfurt before the Second World War but was ultimately forced to flee to safer shores.

On his arrival in Australia as a teenager, he spoke no English, but in a short time he achieved the distinction of being only the second person in Australia to obtain a PHD degree.

Working for free in the 1950's, his passion for studying the wonders of creation led him to discover and successfully develop the world's first antivenins against the Red Back (Black Widow) Spider and the venomous Stone Fish, and he also helped identify the toxin in the lethal Box Jellyfish. As a result, hundreds of lives around the world have been saved over the ensuing decades.

Dr. Wiener regularly studied Gemara, making a yearly pre-Pesach *siyum* for his shul. He was always active in the Australian Jewish community, helping start organizations like Kosher Meals on Wheels and The Council of Orthodox Synagogues.

Never seeking any honor or praise, the honor sought him: Just before his *petirah*, he was awarded the coveted Order of Australia Medal, bestowed upon him by the Commonwealth and the Queen of England for his pioneering research into antivenins.

What requires thought and contemplation for most of us was natural and obvious to Dr. Wiener: that behind every scientific discovery lies Hashem, the Creator of the world. The essence of this book is to teach us and remind us of this.

At the time of publication, Dr. and Mrs. Wiener have over 100 descendants, all *shomer mitzvos* with true *yiras Shamayim* and *ahavas Hashem*, including many *talmidei chachamim* — all this stemming from the way Dr. Wiener saw our wondrous world.

בס"ד

Dear Kids,

Wherever we look, we see the "fingerprints" of man. He's always inventing stuff. When we see a new wristwatch that can not only tell the time, but also tell the temperature, or tell the wearer where he's standing in the city that he lives, or how many steps he's taken today — we're impressed. We know for sure that some smart watch technician has designed that watch. We may never actually meet him, but we know he exists out there somewhere. We have no doubts.

Now hold that thought and let's start again!

Wherever we look, we see the "fingerprints" of Hashem. He's always making stuff. When we see how every single one of His creatures has been made to fit where it lives, we should be even more impressed than we are with a watchmaker. Do we find polar bears living in the desert? Or eagles living under the sea? Those sound like really dumb questions to ask, but guess what? If we don't ask those "dumb" questions, then *we're* really being dumb, because it means we've never really thought deeply about Hashem's creations that are all around us.

Have we ever stopped and wondered why many of the creatures on earth are even more sophisticated than the machines and inventions we have?

Are you ready to open your eyes and your mind and come explore Hashem's creations with me? To see how they can even trump our best inventions? Together we'll see that Hashem is the Divine Inventor. We meet Him all day, every day, all around us. When we explore together, we'll have no doubts. No watchmaker comes even close!

Sitting comfortably? Okay then, let's begin...

Sincerely,

The Torah Vet

GUNS

In the USA, there are almost 270 million guns, and less than 1 million are carried by the police. Close to 33,000 Americans lose their lives each year to gun-related incidents, and an average of 270 people are shot every day!

What a shame that this invention has caused so much destruction.

How does a GUN shoot bullets?

A gun, or pistol, is really like a "house," and the bullet inside it is like a "guest." The gun keeps the bullet nice and "cosy," just like our houses keep us cosy. When it's time for the bullet to leave, the gun just gives it a "shove out the front door." What's really interesting is the bullet. It's just a smooth blob of lead with a coating of hard metal over it. The bullet is wedged into the top end of a metal cylinder called its "shell." The shell has been packed with gunpowder that explodes when it catches fire. At the bottom of the shell is a small disc called a primer that looks like a tiny coin. When a gun's trigger is pulled, a small "hammer" hits that coin-like primer. The primer gives off a spark inside the shell, and this makes the gunpowder explode. The explosion that happens inside the bullet's shell blows the bullet off its top, forcing it out of the gun. The bullet flies so fast (around 1,700 mph, or 2700 km/h), that it can be very destructive or even, *chas v'shalom*, kill. Guns are VERY, VERY dangerous and you should NEVER touch or go near one.

Gunpowder from inside a bullet shell

How was the GUN invented?

Around the 9th century CE, the Chinese discovered the explosive properties of saltpeter (potassium nitrate), a powdery substance mined from the earth. They stuffed it into tubes of bamboo along with bits of iron shrapnel, and placed the bamboo at the ends of their swords to make a very scary flame-thrower. They then found that adding ground-up charcoal gave the explosion more force; they also fashioned metal tubes that were stronger than bamboo, which made the shrapnel fly further and faster. In the 13th and 14th centuries, gunpowder found its way along the famous Silk Route from China to the Middle East and Europe. Before long, handguns, pistols and rifles of many designs were being made to help each of the gentile nations conquer each other's lands.

And what were the Jews doing during these centuries? They were bringing a different explosion to the world: the light of the Rishonim — Rashi, Rashbam, and Rabbeinu Tam in France; Ra'avad, Meiri, and Radak in Provence; Rif, Rambam, Ramban, Rashba, Ran, and Ritva in Spain. The Torah was their occupation, making an explosion of knowledge for the good of mankind.

At marathons, the gun that is fired to start the race fires only blank bullets.

This blank has a case that is pinched closed instead of having a bullet at the head. The primer is the little silver disc seen in the base.

Firing BLANKS
Sometimes guns and pistols are loaded with blank bullets (for example, a start gun used to begin a race). Here the gun is used only to make a loud noise, and no bullet flies out. Blank bullets can be made by stuffing a wad of cottonwool into the top of the bullet shell, instead of a metal bullet. When the primer is whacked by the gun's trigger, the gunpowder explodes and the cottonwool wadding is burnt to ash. It sounds just like a real gun,

Slow motion photo of a bullet ripping through an apple

Can you imagine inventing a
TINY QUARTER-OUNCE GUN
that fires only blanks, but is deadly?

Bullets come in different shapes and sizes. On the right is a bullet cut in half to show the insides.

GIVE IT YOUR BEST "SHOT"!

GUNS

PISTOL SHRIMP — firing blanks that kill!

Hidden away among the corals and sands in the sea is a very special little shrimp that has one small claw and one large, oversized claw — which can be half as long as the whole body of the shrimp. It's called a pistol shrimp for very good reason. This tiny little shrimp (often smaller than a couple of inches) has been given a mighty weapon by Hashem. It doesn't catch its prey with its large claw; rather, it shoots the world's deadliest blank.

One part of its large claw is fixed in place. The other part (called the hammer) is pulled and locked open like the trigger of a gun. It has a swelling on it, called the plunger. When a small fish swims past, the pistol shrimp, hidden from view, releases its hammer, letting it slam down onto the fixed part of the claw — thus snapping the large claw shut and ramming the plunger into a small socket on the fixed part of the claw. What happens next is incredible. The shock wave generated from the claw slamming together is so massive that the sound could burst a person's eardrums. (It measures 220 decibels; human eardrums rupture at 160 decibels.) It also tears a hole in the water, called a cavitation bubble. This hole collapses so fast and so hard that it generates both light and heat. For a fraction of a second, it's as hot as the surface of the sun, which is over 10,000° F (5,500° C)! The shock wave kills or stuns the fish and allows the pistol shrimp to enjoy a well-deserved meal.

The pistol shrimp snaps its claw shut, causing a cavitation bubble to form.

▶ The bubble grows to a **critical size.**

▶ And implodes at a temperature of **10,000 F**

BAM

Let's THINK like the Chachamim!

How could such an oversized claw develop with a hammer that slams shut so hard it makes a deadly "blank bullet" of sound and pressure? Where does this pistol design come from? Who gave this little shrimp the "trick" of developing another pistol claw if it lost the first? Mr. Smith and Mr. Wesson, the developers of a famous handgun, would be very insulted if we said that their guns just developed by accident! So, too, the pistol shrimp is no accident.

FAST FACT: If a pistol shrimp loses its pistol claw, the other small claw begins to grow and change shape until it develops into another pistol!

...and that's as hot as the sun!

לֹא יִשָּׂא גוֹי אֶל גּוֹי חֶרֶב
וְלֹא יִלְמְדוּ עוֹד מִלְחָמָה

No nation will raise a sword against another, and they will learn war no more.

Yeshayahu 2:4

ROCKETS

NASA's Space Shuttle was launched into space by being strapped onto the world's largest rocket fuel tank. Higher than the Statue of Liberty, it helped drive the Space Shuttle into space at a top speed of almost 18,000 mph (29,000 km/h), a speed nine times as fast as the average rifle bullet. Very rarely, rockets can fail, and when they do, it spells disaster for the rocket and, *chas v'shalom*, for the astronauts as well.

How do ROCKET ENGINES work?

Liquid-fuel rocket engines hold two types of liquids in two well-separated tanks. In one tank, the liquid is called the "fuel," and in the other tank, the liquid is called the "oxidizer." Each tank has a turbopump that sucks the liquid from the tank through a tube into a combustion chamber. When the fuel and the oxidizer liquids mix, they react with each other and explode. Massive amounts of energy and gas are released and this gas is forced through the throat of the combustion chamber and out of the rocket's nozzles. The gas rushing out of the nozzles creates "thrust," and this pushes the rocket upward into space. Once rockets are started, they cannot be stopped. The Space Shuttle's engines generated power of over 37 million horsepower. They did this by burning the liquid-fuel at a rate that would drain an average-sized family swimming pool in less than 25 seconds!

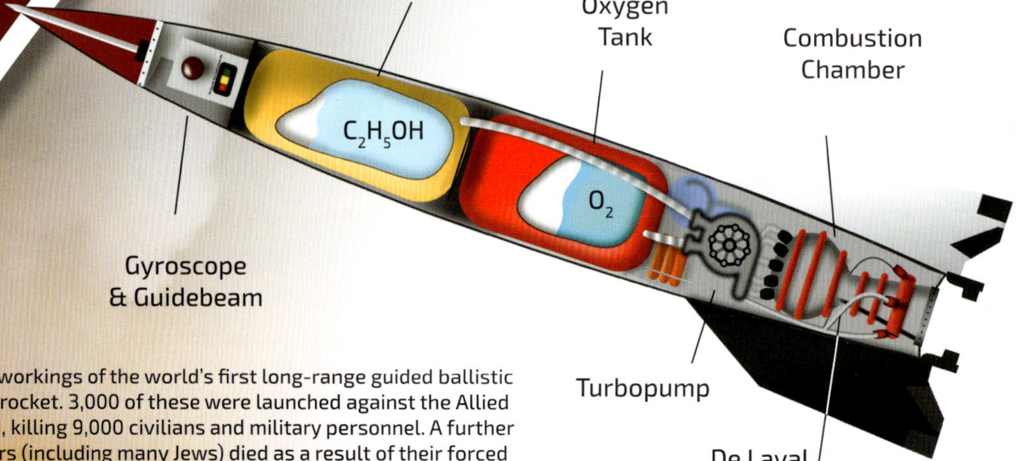

Labels on diagram:
- Liquid Fuel Tank (ethanol and water) — C_2H_5OH
- Liquid Oxygen Tank — O_2
- Combustion Chamber
- Gyroscope & Guidebeam
- Turbopump
- De Laval Nozzle

Diagram of the inner workings of the world's first long-range guided ballistic missile, the Nazi V-2 rocket. 3,000 of these were launched against the Allied forces in World War II, killing 9,000 civilians and military personnel. A further 12,000 forced laborers (including many Jews) died as a result of their forced participation in the production of this rocket.

How was the ROCKET ENGINE invented?

The modern rocket was invented by Robert Goddard in the 1920's. He was the first person to make a rocket that burned liquid fuel in a small combustion chamber and use a de Laval nozzle to help speed up the gas being exhausted. Goddard realised that gas in the combustion chamber is super-hot, but travels slowly. When a de Laval nozzle is attached to the combustion chamber (see the diagram below), the exiting gas is "choked" at the neck of the de Laval nozzle and then rushes past into the wider nozzle. As it does this, it cools down very quickly and instantly accelerates up to supersonic speeds. This doubles the thrust of the rocket.

On 16 March 1926, Robert Goddard launched the world's first liquid-fueled rocket in Auburn, Massachusetts. Over the next twenty years and during World War II, many countries developed versions of rocket engines. Unfortunately, their plan was for rockets to carry bombs. In 1945, German engineer Wernher von Braun, the most infamous Nazi rocket scientist in the world, surrendered to US armed forces. He was taken back to the USA, where he led the "space race" and helped develop the Saturn V rocket that took astronauts Neil Armstrong, Edwin Aldrin and Michael Collins to the moon.

A postage stamp, honoring the work of Dr. Robert Goddard, the inventor of the modern rocket.

Apollo 11 on the way to the first moon landing, being launched on top of the Saturn V Rocket, tallest, heaviest, and most powerful rocket ever used

On the moon — an Apollo astronaut salutes the U.S. flag

ROCKETS

Rocket disasters!

Rockets cost hundreds of millions of dollars to build and need to have many safety features to make sure they don't explode during take-off or flight. No matter how many modifications rocket engineers think of, rockets continue to fail from time to time, showing their design flaws. When they do, we see massive explosions, fireballs, and, lo aleinu, the loss of lives. (Could you imagine how many yeshivos could be supported with the money used to make one rocket?)

On January 28, 1986, a minute after launch of the Space Shuttle Challenger, a large flame plume is visible just above the rocket booster exhaust nozzle. These gases burned through the external tank, which resulted in the loss of the vehicle and its seven-member crew.

Let's THINK like the Chachamim!

It's no secret that the USA made use of a Nazi scientist to develop their rockets. Although we must always be extremely grateful to the countries we live in, we see that the nations of the world seek progress and glory, not moral ideals. Being a Jew is a privilege. We build "rockets" of good behavior and service of Hashem that take us all the way to Gan Eden, not just the moon!

In 2016, Space X's 23-story Falcon 9 rocket, carrying a 6-ton Israeli television and Internet broadcast satellite, exploded before an engine test. There was no loss of life, *baruch Hashem*, but the satellite worth a quarter of a billion dollars went up in smoke.

Now imagine this kind of "rocket":

It doesn't fly anywhere but burns its never-ending supply of fuel for self-defense.

Its fuel tanks are so well insulated that there's NEVER been a failure and a catastrophic explosion.

An unmanned supply rocket for the Space Station explodes as it launches in 2014

It is able to mix fuels and fire its nozzle at will in any direction. It can start and stop its engines up to 500 times a second!

Impossible?
Well, it's here, and Hashem designed it!

IT'S BEST NOT TO **FIRE-UP** THIS CREATURE!

ROCKETS

The SECRET WEAPON of the bombardier beetle

On every continent in the world, except for Antarctica, lives a very special little beetle with an incredible weapon that Hashem has built into its abdomen. When the beetle feels threatened, two rocket-like nozzles eject a foul, boiling chemical plume from the tip of its abdomen with a popping sound. The bombardier points its "rockets" in whatever direction it feels threatened and quite literally burns and boils its victim alive. Remarkably, an extremely advanced rocket engine design has been put into this beetle's body, one that is way smarter than the rockets the scientists have designed.

The bombadier's spray comes out as hot as the water from a boiling kettle!

An ant attacks from the front

The beetle swivels his 'rocket' between his legs and fires forward at the ant

The beetle walks forward, leaving a burned and dying ant behind it

How the BEETLE's rocket-engine works

Hidden deep inside the beetle, are two "fuel" glands that feed two different types of fuel (hydrogen peroxide and hydroquinone) into a large storage tank, where they mix together. Unlike space rockets where the fuels must be kept very separate, the two fuels in the beetle's tank amazingly slosh around and mix together without reacting with each other. If they did, the beetle would literally blow up! When the beetle wishes, it squeezes a jet of this fuel-mix into its own personal combustion chamber near the tip of its abdomen. This chamber is called the vestibule and it is coated with a secretion of chemicals called catalases and peroxidases, which are like a small flame waiting for gasoline to be thrown onto it. In this chamber a violent explosion takes place when the jet of fuel-mix is squeezed into it. Both fuels react instantly with the coating of chemicals and each other. The result is a mixture of boiling hot water that reaches 212° F (100° C), scalding steam under high pressure, and a noxious, irritating chemical called benzoquinone. This boiling concoction explodes out of the beetle's nozzles at a rate of almost 500 pulses per second. The beetle can swivel its nozzles around almost 270 degrees and hold itself dead-still instead of rocketing off from the force of the explosions. Nothing trying to attack the bombardier beetle stands a chance!

Combustion Chamber · Mixing Chamber · Hydroquinone Gland · Explosive Gas · Controller Sphincter Muscle · Hydrogen Peroxide Gland

THE FIREWORKS VIEW HAS GOT TO BE BETTER FROM UP HERE!

שְׁרָצִים אוֹמְרִים:
יְהִי כְבוֹד ה' לְעוֹלָם
יִשְׂמַח ה' בְּמַעֲשָׂיו

The creeping creatures say (Tehillim 104:31), "May the glory of Hashem endure forever; may Hashem rejoice in His works."

Perek Shirah

GPS

Each day, people drive to destinations they've never been to before with the help of a GPS device on their car's dashboard. It tells them where they are, what road they're driving on, in which direction and how fast they're going. There are hundreds of millions of these devices around the world, all working at the same time. What on earth (or in space) tells every GPS where it is?

How does GPS work?

GPS, also known as Global Positioning System, was designed to help travelers navigate (know where they are) on the earth. It has two parts: the GPS receiver and a set of space satellites. The receiver is the touch-screen device on your car's dashboard, and it "speaks" to the twenty-four satellites orbiting the earth. Each one of these satellites weighs up to 4,000 lb (1,800 kg) and measures 17 ft (5 m) across. They all fly in space, 12,000 miles (20,000 km) above the earth at around 8,640 mph (4 km/sec). Their orbits (flight paths) are all different so that anyone with a GPS device anywhere on the entire earth at any time of night or day is in "direct sight" of at least three satellites. So look up! Because right now, there are at least three or more GPS satellites flying in the sky above you.

Your GPS receiver in your car listens for a "song" of computer code from each of the three satellites in sight. This code tells it where the satellites are in space and how far away from your receiver they are. Your GPS receiver can now work out its own exact position on the surface of the earth using a complex calculation called trilateration. Most GPS receivers today are accurate to 66 ft (20 m) almost anywhere on the earth.

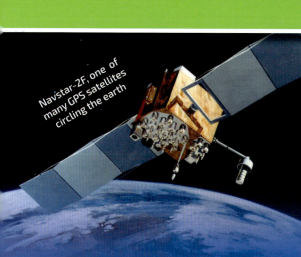

Navstar-2F, one of many GPS satellites circling the earth

GPS satellites form a network that circles the earth, always making sure that at least 3 satellites are in view of your GPS device.

It cost approximately 12 billion dollars to set up the 24 GPS satellites, and it currently costs around 2 million dollars each DAY to run the GPS system. There have actually been 72 GPS satellites launched into space, but most have been retired since they only last approximately 15 years.

Inventor Roger L. Easton

Imagine this kind of GPS system...

What if you had this conversation with GPS inventor **Roger L. Easton**:

"**Sir,** forget the 288,000 lb (130,635 kg) of satellite technology floating above the earth. Please design a system where the GPS receiver...

doesn't need satellites, weighs only one-hundredth of an ounce (1/4 of a gram), and is powered by flowers.

It must be capable of...

navigating a 2,500 mile (4,000 km) journey across two continents and deliver its passenger to a target location of around twelve acres (five hectares) in diameter."

YOU'D NEED THE WEALTH OF A MONARCH TO DESIGN THIS...

GPS

A BUTTERFLY with an incredible compass

The beautiful monarch butterfly starts life as a multicolored caterpillar with yellow, black and white stripes, and a pair of black horns on either end. Since it eats the leaves of the milkweed plant, it concentrates the milkweed's poison into its flesh. The bright stripes warn birds that they shouldn't make a meal of this caterpillar!

After molting (shedding its skin) four times, the caterpillar hangs itself from a branch using a silk thread, and then molts one last time. But instead of shedding the skin, it turns the dead skin around itself into a beautiful green and gold case called a chrysalis. Over the next few weeks, the caterpillar sleeps inside this case, while Hashem creates a wonder…

When it's ready, what chews its way out of the case is not a caterpillar, but rather a magnificent butterfly with black and orange wings.

This is the monarch. Its brain is smaller than a pin-head, yet this butterfly has a very special gift — the gift of GPS.

When the weather in North America and Canada cools during autumn, millions of monarch butterflies leave on an epic journey to avoid the freezing cold winter. The monarchs fly due south to a tiny patch of forest near El Rosario in Mexico. There it's warm and comfortable during winter and they can lay their eggs on pine and oyamel trees. Their journey is over 2,500 miles (4,000 km) long and they need to find a patch of forest no bigger than a few hectares in size. Not a single butterfly lives long enough to make a round trip, which means that no butterfly ever knows the route from memory. It's always their first and last trip. At winter's end, a new generation of monarchs makes the journey back to North America.

The Monarch Butterfly's cocoon — changing into the world's most sophisticated GPS

A monarch caterpillar with its bright warning stripes.

The monarch emerges from its cocoon with built-in GPS.

The monarch feeds exclusively on the nectar of the milkweed flower.

"LOOKS LIKE THE SATELLITE IS LOST!"

Let's THINK like the Chachamim!

Scientists explain this incredible feat of natural GPS by saying that the monarch uses a "time-compensated sun compass"; or when it's cloudy, they think it uses "the polarization of the light" to figure out in which direction they're flying. However you try to explain it, there are two unbelievable things here: (1) Monarch butterflies have a built-in GPS in their brain that is no bigger than a pin-head. (2) Some scientists with a brain weighing 3 lb (1.5 kg) still can't see the miracles of Hashem.

שְׂאוּ מָרוֹם עֵינֵיכֶם וּרְאוּ מִי בָרָא אֵלֶּה

Look up on high and realize Who created these!

Yeshayahu 40:26

THE TASER

It's dark and dangerous! Two police officers enter a jewelry store to catch the thief inside. As they turn a corner, the thief rushes at them with a knife. One of the officers is holding a strange device. He quickly aims and presses its trigger. Two small metal darts shoot out and hit the thief, delivering an electric shock. The thief instantly freezes, drops the knife and falls to the floor, allowing the officers to handcuff him. What electric weapon is this, able to stun its victim so well?

How does a TASER STUN GUN work?

The Taser is a strange, blunt-ended electric gun that doesn't shoot bullets. Rather, it shoots out two small metal electrodes that are shaped like darts. Both darts are connected to the gun by long thin electrical wires that can stretch up to 35 ft (10 m) in length. Rather than police officers shooting a gun that can kill, they shoot criminals with a Taser. When they press the trigger, a small can of compressed nitrogen is activated, which causes the darts to shoot out of the Taser. The darts are barbed like fishing hooks, making them difficult to pull out of clothing. When the darts hit the criminal, an electrical circuit is closed and a "shaped pulse" of electricity flows into the criminal. This electric shock paralyzes the person's nerves and muscles for a short while, allowing the police officers to arrest the criminal without worrying about their own safety.

The Taser has one disadvantage: it can only be used once before its compressed nitrogen cartridge needs replacement.

An illustration of the Taser darts immobilising a criminal

A Taser-like shock device, showing the electric current generated when it is fired

How was the TASER invented?

The Taser was originally developed in 1969 by Jack Cover Jr., a NASA researcher. He wanted to develop a rifle that used an electrical shock rather than bullets. His first model was registered in 1976, but since it used gunpowder to shoot the electric darts, it was considered a firearm. Seventeen years later in 1993, Patrick Smith joined forces with Mr. Cover and developed the first Taser that used tiny canisters of compressed nitrogen. This model was made to stun, not kill. It included an "anti-felon identification (AFID) system" to prevent it from being bought and used by criminals: when fired, it released thousands of tiny papers with the serial number of the Taser gun being used. In this way, it would only be a stun device used by police officers.

A barbed Taser dart stuck to clothing

The Taser X26, issued only to policemen

Now let's imagine this kind of Taser stun gun...

- This stun gun **never** needs reloading of its compressed nitrogen canisters.
- It has **two settings**: one for finding its victim, and one for immobilizing its victim.
- It works at up to 900 volts, which is almost **eight times as powerful** as a US electrical socket.
- And it works **under water!**

WHICH OF HASHEM'S STUNNING CREATURES COULD DO THIS?

THE TASER

Meet the ELECTRIC EEL!

The electric eel grows to 6 ft (2 m) in length and weighs around 44 lb (20 kg). It is found in all the rivers of the Amazon Basin in South America. It's certainly not a kosher fish, as it has no scales. Curiously, it needs to breathe air, coming up to the surface of the water to take a breath every ten minutes before diving into the deep again. The eel has tiny eyes and can't see well. Not only that, the water of the Amazon River is murky like dark tea! It's difficult to see anything in this water.

An eel with an electric personality…

The eel has three special organs in its body that can make electricity: the Hunter's organ, the Sachs organ and the main organ. These organs take up four-fifths of the eel's whole body, and they are made of special muscle cells that can make and store an electric charge. The "electrical" muscle cells are called electrocytes; they are lined up in rows of millions and then stacked, row on top of row, just like the inside of a car battery. So what's the difference between these three electrical organs? Each organ allows the eel to make a different type of electric shock.

In the Sach's organ, the electricity is of a type that allows the eel to swim around in the rivers without bumping into anything (similar to a bat flying in the dark). This is called electrolocation.

The Hunter's organ makes pulses of low voltage electricity. The eel constantly fires off this electric charge as it swims through the water looking for prey to eat. Any hiding fish or crab that is near the eel gets a small electrical shock from this pulse of electricity, which makes it give off a small muscular jolt, just like you would if you got a little shock. When that happens, the electric eel senses the movement of the fish in the water and knows exactly where its prey is!

Now the eel's main organ is discharged. It releases a huge package of electricity into the water — up to 900 volts, which is almost eight times as strong as a power socket in the wall! The electrical shock from the main organ electrocutes the prey and makes them completely paralyzed so that the eel can swim up to them and just swallow them whole.

> **Why does everyone call me an eel?** I'm actually a knifefish, which is a type of catfish. There's only three known electric fish in the world, but clearly I'm the most sophisticated of all!

24

Let's THINK like the Chachamim!

Here is an eel that can make three different types of electricity, one of which is stronger than the electricity of a power socket. It makes it with electrical muscles, and has even been known to electrocute alligators! And just when you think that's incredible, I'll bet you didn't think of this: Hashem gave this eel insulation. It doesn't ever electrocute itself. Now that's a neat trick that only the Borei Olam could "invent"!

The shock delivered by an electric eel is almost eight times as strong as an American power socket.

Diagram of the eel's muscle fibers, zooming in on the rows of electrocytes — muscle cells that make electricity

The electric eel's head has special sensory pits to pick up the tiny vibrations of its prey jerking in the water.

SWIMMING IN THE AMAZON RIVER IS SHOCKING.

וְאֵין עַיִן הָרָע שׁוֹלֶטֶת בָּהֶם

Ayin ha'ra does not rule over fish.

Rashi, Bereishis 48:16

CAMOUFLAGE

A Dassault Mirage jet fighter plane, painted with camouflage

It's early morning, and three terrorists climb quietly out of their tunnel. They're in a grassy field with a few large trees dotted around the entrance. As they tiptoe forward towards the houses of a nearby kibbutz, they don't see the soldiers crouching down directly in front of them. There's a warning shout, then a quick battle and it's over. All the terrorists are caught. How could they not see the men waiting for them? The answer is: camouflage.

What is CAMOUFLAGE?

Camouflage is something used to hide or disguise things so they cannot be seen. It's used mostly by the world's military to disguise their soldiers, equipment and airplanes. Camouflage is accomplished by coloring, painting or covering an item so that it blends in with its surroundings. The most common camouflage item is the uniform that soldiers wear. They have patches of green, tan and brown fabric so that it's difficult to see them, whether they're in fields, forests or mountains. Camouflage clothing is also used by animal hunters and wildlife photographers so that they can get as close to wild animals as possible without being seen.

There's also another kind of camouflage that's even more sophisticated. It's called mimicry. This is when something is *not* disguised so that it can't be seen; rather, the item is disguised to look exactly like something else. It acts as a copy or mimic. A good example of this is when cell phone towers, which usually look like huge, ugly steel poles, are built instead to look just like palm trees.

A cell phone tower designed to mimic a palm tree. You can see the cellular equipment between the fronds.

A field tent camouflaged with branches

A soldier applies camouflage

A hunter dressed in clothing camouflaged to look like leaves or peeling bark

Let's challenge the military...

Imagine asking the US Navy Seals or the Israeli Shin Bet to design a suit for their soldiers that has at least

fifteen different settings, and lets soldiers choose instantly between

camouflage settings

(for example, looking like the sands of the desert)

and mimicry settings

(for example, instantly changing shape to look like a tree or a poisonous snake).

No doubt, the world's top inventors have never and probably will never develop a suit like this.

They're just no match for Hashem!

HOW TO HIDE WITH A BEAK AND 8 ARMS!

CAMOUFLAGE

THE MIMIC OCTOPUS — master of disguise (and surprise!)

In 1998, off the tropical island of Sulawesi in Indonesia, a little octopus with a big talent was discovered. The mimic octopus is one of Hashem's most unique creatures.

It is able to impersonate many other sea animals it lives amongst, instantly changing its shape and color to make itself look like a different animal. If that isn't enough, it can just as quickly change its color to blend in so perfectly with sand, rocks, seaweed or coral that it instantly disappears using perfect camouflage.

The mimic octopus does this by having specialized skin and muscle that can mold itself into many shapes within seconds. Inside its skin, it has special sacs of pigment (like the material in paint) called chromatophores. By rapidly changing the position and shape of these pigment sacs, the mimic can select which color it wants its skin to be. The mimic octopus is currently the only known animal to be able to mimic such a wide variety of animals in such a unique way. There are lots of insects and animals that mimic other animals to stop themselves from being eaten by predators, but their "act" never changes — they always look the same. Good examples are drone flies and bee flies that have black and yellow stripes on their abdomens to mimic bees. However, Hashem has seen fit to make this superb little octopus the master of disguise!

Here are some of the creatures the mimic octopus can imitate:

squid, scorpion fish, banded sea snake, flounder, jellyfish, shrimp, crab, starfish, sea sponge, and eel.

CAMOUFLAGE

Welcome to Hashem's WORLD OF MIMICS

Now if I can sway gently, I'll leaf a positive impression on you.

The leaf fish

A leaf-filled river helps the leaf fish "disappear" and ambush its prey.

The snake caterpillar (pictured here) and a tree snake (below).

Fork-Tailed Drongo

This plain little bird has a neat trick that it plays on meerkats (a type of mongoose). Meerkats are very good at digging juicy insects from the ground and under rocks. Just when they catch their prey, the drongo mimics the meerkat alarm call. All the meerkats drop their prey and scuttle in a flash back into their burrows. The drongo then flies down from its nearby tree to feast on the abandoned insects.

The Leaf Fish

In the streams of the Amazon River lives an incredible little fish that swims head-down in the water, floating just under the surface. It is surrounded by dead leaves that have fallen off the trees above, and it looks remarkably like one of them, with a little stalk on the end of its mouth that looks like a leaf stalk. Other smaller fish that happen to swim by are sucked into the leaf fish's mouth and swallowed in a flash.

Snake Caterpillar
(elephant hawk moth)

This caterpillar has a thick green or brown body with a thinner, longer head that resembles an elephant trunk. When startled by a predator, it pulls its head in towards its fatter body. This makes that last part of its body look exactly like the head of a venomous snake, with body markings that look like a snake's eyes, scaring off the predator.

The Ant Spider

Ants taste horrible to most larger animals, such as birds. So some insects mimic ants to prevent themselves from being eaten. There are many species of spiders that walk on only six of their eight legs by lifting the two front pairs of legs above their heads, mimicking an ant's antennae; they also have elongated bodies so that they look just like ants. This way, they avoid being eaten. There are still other spider species that mimic ants in order to enter ant nests and eat the ants, then leave without the whole colony of ants attacking them.

The Stonefish

The stonefish looks exactly like the rocks, stones and corals amongst which it hides, keeping dead still until a smaller fish swims close by. It then snaps it up in a fraction of a second. Although it is a clumsy swimmer, it has something special to defend itself instead of swimming away — at the bottom of the spines in its main fin (dorsal fin) sit tiny sacs of lethal poison that can even kill a human if he stands on it.

The Owl Butterfly

As its name suggests, this butterfly has very large round black and yellow spots on its gray-brown wings that look exactly like the large eyes of an owl. When a predator (usually a bird or a lizard) swoops down on the butterfly, it folds out its wings and this makes it look just like the face of an owl. The predator is very quickly scared away.

The owl butterfly is so named for its eye-like images on its wings.

The ant spider (pictured here) and a genuine ant (below)

שֶׁמַּטְעֶה רְאִיָּתָם עַד שֶׁרוֹאִים הָרַע כְּאִלּוּ הוּא מַמָּשׁ טוֹב, וְהַטּוֹב כְּאִלּוּ הוּא רָע

The *yetzer ha'ra* distorts matters so that good things look bad and bad things look good.

Mesillas Yesharim, Chapter 3

31

ANTIFREEZE

On a freezing cold winter morning, your father calls your mother from the side of the highway. Halfway to work, his car suddenly made a large noise and then rolled to a stop, steam billowing up from the hood. "I forgot the antifreeze!" he says, sounding rather upset. "I hope it's just a cracked radiator hose!" Mom groans, thinking about the mechanic's bill, while you sit there, wondering what antifreeze is...

What is ANTIFREEZE?

Antifreeze is a chemical that's added to water so that the water won't freeze in the engine. If you put two cups of water overnight in the freezer, one with antifreeze and one without, the one with just water would be ice the next morning, while the other cup with added antifreeze would still be liquid. Why is antifreeze so important? It's because when water freezes into ice, it expands (gets bigger). If this happens inside a tight space, the expanding ice is so strong it can crack or tear almost any container right open! Antifreeze stops this from happening by stopping water from turning into ice.

Antifreeze is used most commonly in car radiators. Since car engines become very hot when they're running, they have a built-in cooling system that uses a flow of water to pull the heat of the engine away from the center so that the engine doesn't overheat and stop working.

Now imagine it's winter and there's no antifreeze in the car's radiator. All that water can freeze over. When water freezes and turns into ice inside the rubber hoses of the radiator, the expanding ice is so strong it can easily crack or tear the hose. It's even possible for the water inside the steel block of the engine to crack the whole engine block open when it turns into ice. The next morning, once the engine is started and warms up, all the ice turns back into water and then pours out of the cracked hose or engine. Before long, there's no water left in the radiator and the car engine can overheat and become badly damaged.

Since beer is mostly water, a bottle of beer can explode if it freezes.

When water freezes in pipes, it expands, This causes pressure so strong that it can crack the pipe and ooze out, as it has done here.

Antifreeze is often colored to warn that it's toxic. Here it's seen glowing green in the radiator.

Dangerous chemicals

Antifreeze stops water from expanding in freezing weather and rupturing its container, but antifreeze itself is very dangerous! The most common type of antifreeze used in cars is called ethylene glycol. If it is swallowed, it can cause vomiting, headaches and eventually death. Kids should NEVER play with antifreeze or any other chemicals that are found in the garage.

Anti-Freeze & Summer Coolant
Contains: Ethylene Glycol

✗ **HARMFUL**

Harmful if swallowed. If swallowed, seek medical advice immediately and show this container or label. Do not induce vomiting. Avoid contact with skin and eyes. Wash hands after use. Keep container clearly labelled. Keep out of the reach of children.

A British warning label for antifreeze.

Could you ever imagine a use for **ANTIFREEZE** in a **LIVING THING?**

THE ANSWER IS JUST A **HOP, SKIP** & **JUMP** AWAY...

ANTIFREEZE

Hashem's astounding WOOD FROG

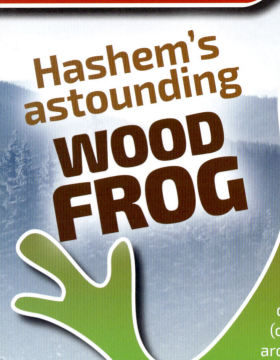
A wood frog frozen on the surface of a lake

The wood frog

In Canada, Alaska and the Northeastern US lives a little brown frog with a very big talent. In late autumn, when squirrels and bears are getting ready to hibernate, the wood frog is doing no such thing. He keeps himself busy, hopping around and feeding in the soil and leaf litter. Somehow, even when the temperature dives down towards freezing, Hashem has built into the frog's muscles and other tissues an amazing "turbo-drive" that lets the frog burn his fuel (called ATP) and have energy to move around, when other animals are already sound asleep in their dens and caves.

And if that isn't amazing enough, the wood frog also has a type of built-in antifreeze. As the weather turns even colder and everything becomes iced over, the frog's body starts making massive amounts of urea and glucose. These two natural chemicals build up inside the tissues and the blood, and act as cryoprotectants (this is another word for antifreeze). This means that they stop icicles from forming deep inside the frog's body, and they also reduce the size of the icicles forming in the muscles, skin and eyes which are more superficial. The tinier the ice crystals, the less damage they do to the tissues. Up to two-thirds of the frog's body eventually does freeze solid. The frozen "frogsicle" stops breathing, its heart stops beating, and only a very small amount of its vital organs remain unfrozen deep inside the center of its body. It stays outside on the ground, in the howling wind and cold of winter.

In the spring as the ice and snow melts, the frozen frog slowly thaws, its heart starts beating, it starts breathing again and comes back to life — a miracle of Hashem's design.

ANTIFREEZE

Hashem's INCREDIBLE FROGS

The flying frog displays his massive webbed toes that act as parachutes.

The Flying Frog

In the jungles of Malaysia and Borneo lives a super little frog that thinks it's a bird! Wallace's flying frog has thin skin stretched out between all of its toes. When it leaps off a tree, it spreads its feet out wide, catching the wind in its webbings much like a glider or parachute; it then simply glides from tree to tree. This frog also just happens to have oversized toe pads to help it stick to tree trunks and to land softly.

The Skin Blister Frog

The Surinam frog (it's actually a toad) is the world's flattest amphibian; it looks like it's been squished by a steamroller. Its flat shape together with its brown skin helps it hide among the leaves and plant debris in the streams it lives in. But this amazing amphibian has another neat trick up its sleeve: after laying its eggs, it sticks the eggs to its back. The skin becomes soft and grows right over the eggs, forming protective pockets over them, so the frog's back looks like a honeycomb. The tadpoles grow inside these pockets and emerge as toadlets after 20 weeks.

A toad specimen showing its eggs brooding inside the skin of its back

Babies hatching from a Surinam toad

The Poison Dart Frog

Deep in the jungles of Central and South America lives a family of extraordinary frogs. Each member shares two characteristics: they have brilliant warning colors and patterns on their skins, and they're potently toxic to any animal that decides to eat them. Native South American Indians have pressed their blowdarts against the skins of these frogs before using them to hunt. Once the dart is shot into an animal, the animal rapidly becomes paralyzed. The most toxic of these beautifully colored frogs is the golden poison frog (Phyllobates terribillis). Its rich yellow-gold skin contains enough poison to kill 10,000 mice, or 20 humans, or 2 African elephants! Scientists think that the poison in the frog's skin builds up from toxins in the ants that these frogs eat. But how do they explain that the toxins are harmless to these frogs, but rapidly kill other animals? Only Hashem could design these frogs this way.

The Turtle Frog

In the sandy coastal plains of southwest Australia lives an unusual frog-out-of-water. The turtle frog is a large, fat pink frog with a tiny head that looks more like a turtle without a shell! It lives in underground burrows and chambers in sandy soil, which it digs out using its unusually fat and powerful front legs. (Frogs usually dig backwards with their back legs; the turtle frog digs forward with its front legs.) It burrows deep into the sand, sniffing out termite nests, since it eats mainly termites. Interestingly, it lays its eggs underground; they hatch into fully developed frogs after six months (without a true tadpole phase).

Golden poison dart frog

Strawberry poison dart frog

ANTIFREEZE

...even more INCREDIBLE FROGS

The Baby-Swallowing Frog

The southern gastric brooding frog from northern Australia is a parent that has a very strange way of "bringing up" its kids! It was first discovered in 1972 in creeks and ponds in the Queensland rainforests. First the mother frog swallows her eggs; then her digestion grinds to a halt and she stops eating. During this time, the eggs hatch and tadpoles develop in her stomach, which has become a warm little pond. Six to eight weeks later, once the tadpoles have developed into fully formed little froglets, the mother frog opens her mouth and vomits her babies up, which then happily hop away! This incredible frog is most probably extinct, as it was last seen in the wild in 1981.

The Cocoon Frog

Believe it or not, this is a frog that can live in the bone-dry desert! Commonly known as the water-holding frog, this Australian frog burrows underground and can remain "asleep" for more than five years if it needs to survive a drought. It does this by storing large amounts of water in its bladder, and by forming a "cocoon" of mucus around itself to reduce loss of water. The outside of the cocoon hardens, while inside the frog remains moist. This frog will only come up to the surface to eat after an outbreak of heavy summer rains. Water-holding frogs were traditionally used by the Aboriginal peoples in Australia as a source of drinking water. They would dig up the frogs, and then gently squeeze the water from them before letting them go unharmed.

Gastric brooding frog, with a baby emerging from its mouth

Gastric brooding frog, showing how its stomach acts as a "pool" in which its tadpoles develop

The Glass Frog

Glass frogs are tree frogs that are active at night and live deep in the forests of South America. Hashem has given them translucent skin on the underside of their bodies. This means that you can see right through their skin like a piece of glass so that their internal organs — even a beating heart — can be seen. Their glass-like skin helps them blend in with the leaves so that they can't be seen by predators.

A view of the glass frog from underneath, showing its organs through its transparent skin

"THAT'S THE LAST TIME I "CHILL OUT" WITH A WOOD FROG!"

צְפַרְדֵּעַ אוֹמֶרֶת:
בָּרוּךְ שֵׁם כְּבוֹד
מַלְכוּתוֹ לְעוֹלָם וָעֶד

The frog says, "Blessed is the Name of His glorious kingdom forever."

Perek Shirah

SPORTS CARS

World's first automobile

One hundred and thirty eight years ago, Carl Benz designed the world's first automobile. It had three bicycle-like wheels and reached a top speed of a very speedy 12 miles per hour (20 km/hr). Fast forward to today, and we think we're smart because our sports cars can accelerate from zero to sixty miles per hour (0–100 km/hr) in three seconds! Well, Hashem has some surprises for us...

Carl Benz

The quest for SPEED

For over a century, the nations of the world have spent much time, money and effort in perfecting the car and trying to make it travel faster and faster. *Baruch Hashem*, we can take advantage of this technology, and this allows us to get from place to place without wasting time. In truth, from a Torah perspective, if the car (along with other modern inventions of transport) was only invented to save a single *talmid chacham* some precious time to learn and serve Hashem, for that alone it would have been worth it. Car designers would never see it that way. The faster and more powerful a car is, the better; and there are many people who have been known to spend millions of dollars just because they want to own the fastest or most prestigious sports car in the world!

The average sports car has 600 horsepower. That's the strength of all the horses pictured here, multiplied by 30.

Not every car is a sports car. To qualify, the sports car must have a number of outstanding characteristics. Here are some of them:

What makes SPORTS CARS so fast?

Light weight

The less the car weighs, the faster its engine can propel it. Often the outer body of the sports car is made of lightweight materials such as carbon-fiber, rather than sheet metals which are heavier. Unnecessary switches and dials are removed and even the car's pedals are drilled out to make them more lightweight.

Aerodynamic

Cars need to break through the air as they go faster. The lower and sleeker they are, the more effectively the wind is "sliced" and pushed out of the way. This makes acceleration easier.

A low, sleek car design makes for good aerodynamics.

Carbon fiber weave is very strong and very light — here it is on a sports car steering wheel.

Road Contact

Sports cars always have very wide (thick) wheels that have low-profile tires. This means there's more contact between the car and the road, and it means the force of its powerful engine can be directed more effectively onto the road to push the car forward using traction.

A wide wheel with a low-profile tire makes for better road contact.

Horse power

Most car technology today is focused on the engine. By reducing its weight and increasing its power, more rotational force (torque) can be used to rotate the wheels around at a faster rate. If a sports car has 600 horsepower, it means that the engine produces the same rate of work as 600 horses!

SPORTS CARS

WEIRD Car Facts

The world's smallest car, the 1964 Peel P50

Smallest

The Peel P50 is the world's smallest car. It has three wheels and is classed as a microcar. It was manufactured from 1962 to 1965 by the Peel Engineering Company on the Isle of Man in the United Kingdom. In 2010, it was entered into the Guinness World Records as the smallest production car ever made.

Fastest

Currently, the world's fastest production car that is legally allowed to be sold and registered with a number plate is the **Bugatti Veyron Super Sport**. Only 30 cars have been produced (all by hand), and they have a top speed of 257 mph (415 km/h).

The world's fastest sports car Bugatti Veyron Super Sport

Longest

The American Dream was built in California in the late 1980's. It was a massive custom-made limousine that measured 100 ft long (30 m), ten times the length of an average car! It had 26 wheels, a jacuzzi, king-sized water bed, and even a helicopter landing pad.

The world's longest car is currently rusting in pieces (see below) in New York. It was all for show anyhow, as it could not turn well, and was transported in parts and reassembled wherever it went.

42

Most Expensive

In 2014, a very big spender purchased at auction a **1962 Ferrari 250 GTO** for $38,115,000 (over thirty-eight million dollars), the single largest amount ever paid for a car. The world's most expensive production car will soon be the **Aston Martin Red Bull 001** that will come with a mere four million dollar price tag.

Stop and think about this for a second: How much good could come from a person having

Let's THINK like the Chachamim!

a four-million dollar piece of metal parked in his garage? Yet how much good could come from a person having four million dollars invested in mitzvos, say a yeshiva, *kollel* or charity?

The best sports cars can accelerate **FROM 0 TO 60MPH (0–100 KM/HR) IN AROUND 3 SECONDS!**

Well that's a silly thing to brag about…

IT'S HASHEM'S **"ROADSTER"** THAT HAS A REAL NEED FOR SPEED…

SPORTS CARS

CHEETAH –
the creature that **runs on air,** not land…

The cheetah is the undisputed king of speed.

Similar to Ferraris, McLarens and Lamborghinis, the cheetah is very aerodynamic, with a very small, streamlined head, flattened rib cage and long legs, **so it can cut through the air like an arrow.**

This magnificent member of the cat family has very impressive acceleration. In only three strides it accelerates from zero to sixty miles an hour (0–100 km/hr) and it does this in less than three seconds. Head to head with all the world's top sports cars, the cheetah comes out on top. How does it do this? Hashem has quite simply designed it for speed. It has a very slim, lightweight body frame (weighing only 125 lb), which means its long powerful muscles can focus entirely on propulsion.

The cheetah is so successful at speed that it **catches and kills its prey in one out of every two animals it chases.** Compare this to a lion, which has a kill rate of only one in six animals it chases.

The cheetah can stretch its front and back legs very far out from its body, and then bring them back in and overlap them underneath its body. All this makes for **a stride length of an amazing 25 feet!** That's the same as four tall men lying head to toe. Twice during each stride, all four feet of the cheetah are off the ground — its feet actually spend more time suspended in the air than in contact with the earth.

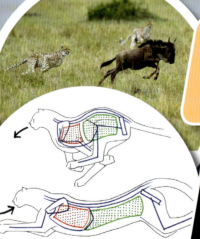

The cheetah has such a huge stride that it forces air in an out of its lungs when running.

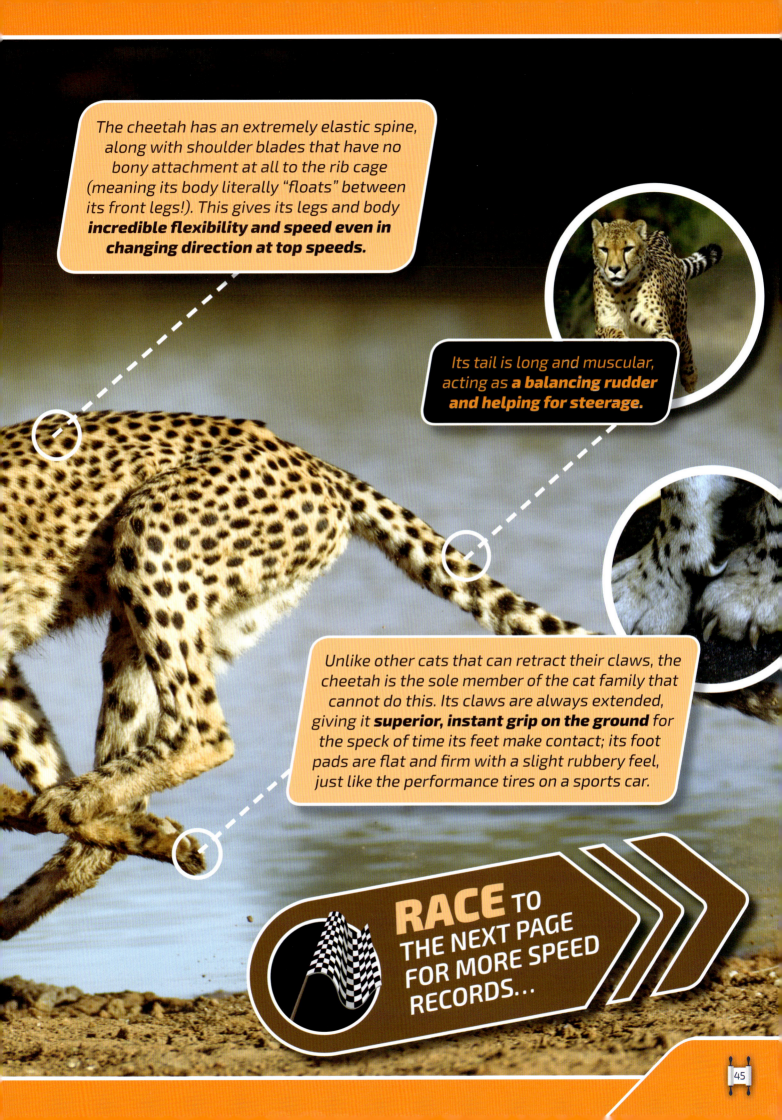

The cheetah has an extremely elastic spine, along with shoulder blades that have no bony attachment at all to the rib cage (meaning its body literally "floats" between its front legs!). This gives its legs and body **incredible flexibility and speed even in changing direction at top speeds.**

Its tail is long and muscular, acting as **a balancing rudder and helping for steerage.**

Unlike other cats that can retract their claws, the cheetah is the sole member of the cat family that cannot do this. Its claws are always extended, giving it **superior, instant grip on the ground** for the speck of time its feet make contact; its foot pads are flat and firm with a slight rubbery feel, just like the performance tires on a sports car.

RACE TO THE NEXT PAGE FOR MORE SPEED RECORDS...

SPORTS CARS

"KIPPAH'S ARE SURE BUILT FOR LIMUD HATORAH, NOT CONVERTIBLES."

The FAST...

The Peregrine Falcon

The peregrine falcon snacking on a pigeon

This is the fastest animal in the air, and also in the entire animal kingdom. When it hunts for prey, it flies very high up in the sky. Hashem has given it a light underbelly, making it harder to spot against the surrounding sky and clouds. Once it locks onto its prey (usually other birds like pigeons), it literally dive-bombs them like a missile. When it does this, it can cut through the air on a downward swoop, reaching an incredible speed of 200 mph (320 km/hr). It kills its prey in mid-air, flying away to feast on it later. You can read more about the peregrine falcon on page 68.

The South Californian Mite

Yes, you read correctly. Paratarsotomus macropalpis (say *that* fast) is a tiny insect that is often seen darting along sidewalks and living among rocks. It has an impressive length of less than 0.04 in (1 mm), but its speed is truly remarkable. When all animals' speeds are compared to each other by how many of its own body lengths it runs in a second (for example, a cheetah runs at 16 of its own body lengths per second), this little mite runs at a speed of 322 body lengths per second. If a human being ran that fast, our speed would be 1,300 mph (2,092 km/h) which is close to Mach 2, or the same speed as a jet fighter plane! It is the fastest known living thing on earth.

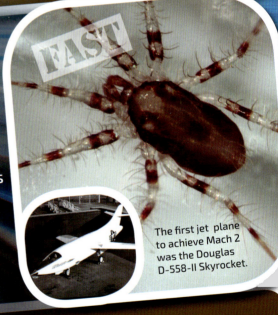

The first jet plane to achieve Mach 2 was the Douglas D-558-II Skyrocket.

The Black Marlin

The black marlin is heavier than Khalid-Bin-Mohsen-Shaari, who was 1,340 lb (610 kg) at his peak weight.

In the oceans, the fastest creature by far is the black marlin. It's a massive fish, weighing in at 1,650 lb (750 kg) and measuring up to 15 ft (4.5 m). It is found in the Indian and Pacific Oceans and it has been recorded by professional fisherman as unwinding their fishing line at 80 mph (129 km/h). That's faster than your parent's car is allowed to drive on the highway, and that's through water! Also known as the swordfish, it has a long, sword-like bill that it uses to hunt and kill its prey.

The Three-Toed Sloth

Being the slowest mammal on earth isn't easy. This large cat-sized creature lives almost its entire life hanging upside down from a tree branch using its three large hook-like claws. It moves so slowly that it usually never ventures further than the few trees it calls home. Sloths come down out of their trees once a week to "use the bathroom" on the forest floor. They spend as little time on the ground as possible since they cannot walk at all, only crawl on their bellies. The hair on their bellies actually grows backward and often looks green because it grows a layer of algae on it. Hashem has built them so perfectly for an upside-down life that their skeletons have been found hanging from branches after they've died.

The Banana Slug

Forget snails; this yellow-colored slug is so slow that it moves at 0.0009 in (0.0023 cm) per second, or a paltry 3.15 in (8 cm) per hour (or just 2 ft [1 m] per day)! The banana slug also has the dubious honor of being the second largest slug in the world, sometimes growing up to 10 in long (25 cm), and it has only one lung. It is particularly fond of hunting and eating mushrooms, which luckily don't move very fast either!

Lichens

Have you ever noticed those flat, ruffled patches of color that seem to be growing on rocks and sidewalks? They're sometimes light green, brown or orange. Well, believe it or not, those patches are alive! They're a type of a fungus, and their color comes from algae or cyanobacteria that live inside the fungus. Some large patches of lichen are estimated to be a few thousand years old because they grow at the incredibly slow rate of only 0.04 in (1 mm) per year!

...and the SLOW

דֶּרֶךְ מִצְוֹתֶיךָ אָרוּץ

On the way of Your mitzvos, I will run.

Tehillim 119:32

WELDING HELMETS

Two pieces of metal joined together by welding

All the things in your home made of metals are "glued" together by welding. To join such hard pieces together, welding needs concentrated heat to melt the metal. When this happens, an instant burst of very bright light is made. It's impossible to see anything in this light, and it can be very dangerous to your eyes. So what do welders use to protect their eyes and see what they're doing?

What happens when you WELD?

In metal fabrication businesses around the word, workmen join pieces of metal together using a special electrical welding gun that has a welding stick at its end. When the welding stick touches the metal, a massive electrical current creates instant heat, light and sparks that melt the metal pieces and "glue" them together. The welding stick itself melts slowly as it is being used, and it helps protect the "metal glue" joining the metal pieces together by coating it with a substance called slag. The light and sparks that are made during welding are so bright that it's impossible to see what you're doing, and the light can burn the front of an onlooker's eyes (the cornea) or even burn the back of the eye (the retina). When this happens, one suffers from a very painful condition called arc eyes, and in some severe cases, if the retina of the eye is badly damaged, it can even *chas v'shalom* cause blindness. To prevent this, the welder wears a special helmet.

How do WELDING HELMETS work?

To protect a welder's eyes and face, he wears a helmet that has a small viewing window to allow him to see. The window is made of extremely dark glass, so dark in fact that you can't see a thing through it if you pull the helmet down when you're not welding. So the typical welder's helmet usually sits like a cap on top of the welder's head until he's ready to weld. After the welder aims his welding stick on the right spot, he nods his head forward so the mask falls down into place, and then he starts welding. The super-bright, dangerous light and sparks that are made now allow him to see what he's doing through the dark glass, which also protects his eyes from damage. New technology helmets now have a glass viewing window that is completely clear so a welder can keep it on even when he's not welding. The glass has a built in layer called an LCD electronic shutter. It senses immediately when the welding starts and darkens instantaneously to protect the eyes. When the welding stops, the LCD shutter switches itself off and the viewing window is once again clear!

Speedglas auto-darkening helmet

Arc eyes caused by welding without a helmet

LET'S SEE ANOTHER PHOTOSENSITIVE TECHNOLOGY...

WELDING HELMETS

Man wearing glasses made of photosensitive lenses

Other PHOTOSENSITIVE technologies

Some people have eyes that are very sensitive to daylight. The UV (ultraviolet) light rays damage their eyes. Normal life becomes difficult as they keep on having to switch from glasses to sunglasses when going outside. This began changing in the 1960's, when a man named Roger Araujo invented the photochromic lens while working for Corning Glass Works. Araujo found that if one embeds microscopic crystals of silver-halides (a molecule of silver joined to a molecule of chlorine) onto a glass surface, the glass darkens in sunlight and becomes clear again when indoors. Today we use this technology in eyeglasses with transition lenses.

WELDING HELMETS

Hashem's amazing COLOR-CHANGING creatures

The Chameleon

Here is a type of lizard that Hashem has jam-packed with many incredible abilities. Just one of these talents is its knack for changing color. The chameleon's skin can change from green through yellow, brown and red, and in varying patterns too. It does this in order to blend in with its background (a type of camouflage). Its color also changes with its mood. Many chameleons change their skin color to a rich red when they're angry, puffing their throats out and hissing as a warning to other animals. When they're among dead foliage or on branches, their skin color is a patterned brown, and when they're hiding among the leaves of trees, they have a bright green color, helping them blend in with their environments. Chameleons are found mainly in sub-Saharan Africa and on the island of Madagascar.

Around the gray circle is a mere sampling of the countless color shades a chameleon's skin can turn!

How does their skin work?

The top layer of a chameleon's skin contains a fine web of extremely tiny crystals of guanine (something found in everyone's DNA). The chameleon's nerves can excite this web, which changes the spacing between the crystals. Depending on how far apart or close together the guanine crystals are, the skin will absorb some wavelengths of light and reflect others. (Think of a prism which instead of reflecting all the colors of the rainbow when light shines through it, can decide to sometimes only let red light through, or at other times only green light through.) This miracle of engineering means that when the chameleon is relaxed, the crystals reflect blue and green light, but when excited reflect yellow, orange and red.

WELDING HELMETS

AND MORE COLOR-CHANGING CREATURES

The Cuttlefish

This is not a fish at all, but rather an odd shaped mollusc that lives in the sea. Other creatures in the mollusc family include the octopus, slug and snail. Cuttlefish can change the shape and color of their skin in very dramatic fashion, sometimes changing color and shape within a second or two. Hashem has given them not one, but *three* ways of doing this, as their skin has three layers. The topmost layer contains cells called chromatophores. They look like a stretchy sac filled with hundreds of granules of pigments. Some sacs are filled with red granules, some with yellow and orange granules and some with brown and black granules. Each sac has a folded curtain-like covering on top; tiny muscles and nerves surround the sac, like the springs at the edge of a trampoline. When the cuttlefish wants, it activates the muscles to different chromatophore sacs. The curtain-like covering is drawn back, the sac is pulled flat, and the beautiful colored pigment granules can now be seen. The middle and deepest layer of skin contain special cells called iridophores and leukophores. Both these cells have microscopic stacks of crystal plates. Each plate reflects different rays of light like a mirror. The colors from these cells have a metallic look and can vary greatly like all the colors of the rainbow.

Cuttlefish skin: The chromatophores are the brown dots. Iridophores are metallic gold patches underneath.

Chromato-, leuko-, and iridophores — three cuttlefish skin cells that create infinite skin patterns and colors

The Golden Tortoise Beetle

This beetle is around one-fifth of an inch (5 mm) long and is commonly found in the Americas. Most adult beetles are a brilliant shiny gold color, with the edges of their shells being transparent. Scientists aren't completely sure how this beetle changes color, but if disturbed, its shell changes from gold to yellow or red as a warning. One theory is that this color change happens when the beetle sucks out all the extra fluid stored in the topmost layers of its shell. When the danger passes, it rehydrates its shell (lets moisture flow back into all layers of its shell) and this changes its shell color back to gold.

Let's THINK like the Chachamim!

Many wonderful creatures with tiny brains or no brains at all can change their colors, telling other animals how they're feeling, warning them that they're toxic or harmful, or blending into their backgrounds for camouflage. Just how do all these different pigments and complex ways of changing color come into being, all perfectly matched for the creature and for the place where it lives? It can only be the hand of Hashem!

Every Jew is a unique gem with his own distinct color and beauty.

Rav Dan Segal
shlita

SUNSCREEN

The Negev in the summer at midday: the sun's ultraviolet rays are so strong they can cause severe sunburn in just a few minutes, even when it's cloudy. Hikers need to wear wide-brimmed hats, clothing to cover exposed skin, and sunglasses. For the skin on their faces, they need to smear on a thick layer of sunscreen cream. Without it, their faces would toast, blister and burn.

Boy having sunscreen applied

Sunburned skin

How does SUNSCREEN work?

Not all of the sun's rays are harmful. The rays we're concerned with are called ultraviolet rays. Ultraviolet rays are actually invisible to your eyes, but the damage they cause can be seen when a person's skin gets sunburned. Sunscreen (also known as sunblock) is a substance that is mixed into a "base" of oil or cream. This is smeared onto the skin to prevent sunburn. The sunscreen molecules used today are called "bioadhesive nanoparticles" and they are special because they stick to the outermost layers of skin that are the least sensitive. There, they act like sentries, not allowing the very dangerous ultraviolet rays to burn your cells. They do this by "swallowing" the ultraviolet rays and "spitting them out" as harmless heat waves. The most commonly used sunscreen substances are oxybenzone, titanium oxide and zinc oxide (say those words fast!). No matter how good these sunscreen "sentries" are, they still need to be smeared onto exposed skin every hour or two. The best sunscreen creams have an SPF (Sun Protection Factor) of 50+. This means that when it's on your skin, it will protect you for 50 times longer than without any sunscreen. Although this sounds like a lot of protection, a responsible person will stay out of the sun or make sure to always smear more sunscreen on, especially after swimming.

How was SUNSCREEN invented?

People have tried many remedies since ancient times to protect their skins from the sun. The ancient Greeks and Egyptians used extracts of rice and jasmine plants mixed with olive oil. The first sunscreen product that was made for sale was in 1936. It was developed by the founder of L'Oreal, French chemist Eugène Schueller. Strangely, the most popular sunscreen during World War II was developed by an airman in the US military. Benjamin Green called his product "Red Vet Pet," short for Red Veterinary Petrolatum. It was a sticky, greasy red-colored jelly that actually didn't work that well. Water-resistant sunscreens that stick to skin even when swimming were introduced in 1977. Nowadays, most research has focused on making spray-on, very high SPF sunscreens that are ultra long lasting, waterproof and safe even for babies.

IMAGINE BEING BORN WITH BUILT-IN SUNBLOCK?

SUNSCREEN

The hippo

The hippopotamus is a strange creature indeed. Its name means "horse of the river," and it's a very good description of this cute, but very large, very fat and, surprisingly, very dangerous animal that spends most of its life in the rivers of Africa. Hippos look like massive red-brown barrels with four stubby legs. They weigh 1.5 tons on average, although some males have been known to grow to 3 tons (7000 lbs)! Although they look clumsy, they can run at almost 19 mph (30 km/hr) on land, and can "swim" incredibly fast (actually they run along the bottom of the river). They have massive jaws that are able to open almost 180 degrees and although they only eat grass, they have four ferocious canine teeth — tusks that can grow as large as 20 in (50 cm). Their jaw power is so strong that it has been measured at almost 2000 lb of pressure per foot. They use these tusks to fight with each other and defend their river territory. Hashem has designed them in the most ingenious way for their life in the water. Their eyes, ears and nostrils are positioned high up on the roof of their skulls. This means that these organs stay above the surface of the water while the rest of their body submerges. This allows them to patrol their patch of river without being easily seen. Their skin is bare with almost no hair at all, and is a glistening chocolate-brown to purple color on top, and a reddish-brown to pink color on its belly and legs. Their skin is also incredibly thick, almost 2 in (6cm) thick, compared to human skin, which is only 0.07 in (2 mm) thick. This protects the hippo in its underwater world, since most of the rivers it lives in are also home to the crocodile.

Hippo skull showing the size of the canine teeth

A hippo's eyes, ears and nostrils are built on top so it can see, smell and hear while in the water.

With a mouth like this, it's no wonder the hippo can be so dangerous.

KEEP YAWNING... KEEP YAWNING.

Don't sweat it, hippo!

But how does a hippo keep from getting sunburned if it has bare skin? A crocodile has thick, horny scales, and lions have thick fur to protect their skin from the sun — but the hippo's skin is soft and smooth. The amazing answer is that hippos are the only creature known to produce their own sunscreen. Special pores, peppered right across their whole body, produce a substance known as "blood-sweat" because of its red color. This oily secretion is neither blood nor sweat, and when it's first secreted, is clear. Within a few minutes it changes color to a deep rich red and spreads across the skin, giving the hippo some of its color. The blood-sweat contains two natural sunscreens — a red pigment (hipposudoric acid) and an orange pigment (norhipposudoric acid). The two pigments are highly acidic compounds that "swallow" ultraviolet light, creating a natural sunscreen. They have another incredible function — they prevent the growth of disease-causing bacteria on the skin, making the "blood-sweat" a natural antibiotic as well.

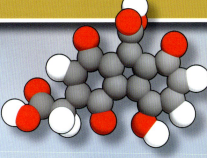

A diagram of hipposudoric acid, the molecule that's the Hippo's natural sunscreen

Hippopotamus showing secretion of sun screen liquid from sweat glands resembling blood

Let's THINK like the Chachamim!

Why don't the lion and crocodile have skins that make blood-sweat, a natural sunscreen? Why isn't the lion's skin two inches thick and why doesn't the lion have its eyes, ears and nostrils positioned on the top of its head? Think about where Hashem put the lion to live, and where He made the hippo's home — in the water. Every part of the hippo's body was planned for where it lives because there is only one planner: Hashem!

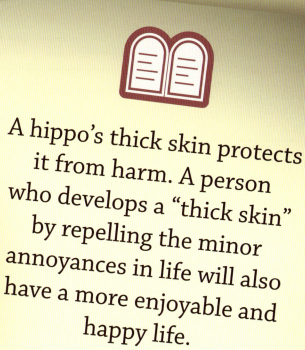

A hippo's thick skin protects it from harm. A person who develops a "thick skin" by repelling the minor annoyances in life will also have a more enjoyable and happy life.

Rav Avigdor Miller zt"l

THERMAL IMAGING

During outbreaks of deadly viruses, many airports around the world have special screening monitors at passport control that "watch" every person traveling. They let out a warning if someone walking past is unwell with a fever. That person may have a virus that could spread to everyone on the plane and into the country where the plane lands. How does this monitor tell who has a fever?

How does THERMAL IMAGING work?

Normal cameras "see" the light waves that we can see with our eyes. The shortest light waves are colored violet, which is like purple. The longest light waves we can see with our eyes are colored red. When waves of light are longer than red, we can't see them with our eyes but they're there, and they're called infra-red light rays. A thermal imaging camera can detect them. It has a special lens like a normal camera, but instead of being made of glass that blocks infrared rays, it's made of sapphire crystal, which lets infrared rays pass through it. The camera's detector can tell the amount of infrared light rays that are coming from any place, and whether they are "hotter" or "colder" (longer wavelength or shorter wavelength). The screen on a thermal imaging camera shows two things: an image of an object or person, and the temperature of that object or person. Not only are these cameras useful at airports, but they are also used in night-vision goggles and telescopes to help soldiers see in pitch darkness, and can even help builders tell where heat is escaping from a building.

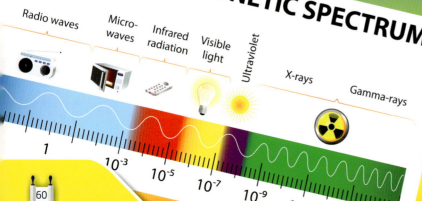

THE ELECTROMAGNETIC SPECTRUM

A graph showing all detectable light rays. Only the yellow section shows light rays visible to our eyes.

Mobile thermal imaging camera

Kálmán Tihanyi, inventor of the infrared camera

How was THERMAL IMAGING invented?

In 1929, Hungarian physicist Kálmán Tihanyi invented the first infrared-sensitive electronic camera that allowed for night vision for anti-aircraft defense in Britain. Since that time, other companies, such as Texas Instruments and Honeywell, developed these cameras further, and in the past thirty years many companies that develop defense technology (equipment sold to the army, air force and navy) have made advances in "smart vision" microchip processing. This allows newer infrared cameras to display the infrared rays more realistically so that it looks like the form and shape of the object it is sensing.

Thermal imaging at passport control

Enhanced night vision camera

Nightvision as seen though goggles; it is pitch black without the goggles.

Imagine having **A SECOND SET OF EYES** *just for thermal imaging!*

CAN YOU GUESS WHO CAN **SSSSSEE** SO MUCH MORE?

THERMAL IMAGING

The viper's night vision apparatus

Vipers (along with pythons and boas) have holes on either side their faces called pit organs. These sit just in front of their eyes; Hashem has given the pit organs an amazing membrane stretching across inside it that can detect infrared radiation. At night in the pitch darkness where no other animals can see, the pit organs allow snakes to "see" an image of their predator or prey — just like an infrared camera does. This gives them an extra set of "eyes."

Incredibly, the pit organ membrane is only activated by temperatures higher than about 82° F (28° C), which is approximately the temperature that a snake would detect from a mouse or a squirrel about a meter away. What the pit organ therefore does is help the snake "profile" its dinner! The snake's brain makes a picture of the size, shape and distance of its prey and allows it to wait patiently or creep up to its meal. Since most of a snake's hunting is done at night when mice and other small mammals are actively foraging for food, having a built-in infrared camera is a huge gift from Hashem.

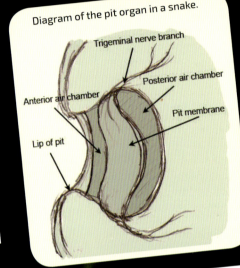

Diagram of the pit organ in a snake.

Eyelash vipers (bothriechis schlegelii), are well-known for their aggression and lightning fast strikes. It's pit organ is the large hole located just to the right of the eye (before the small nostril).

Albino Burmese pythons are not poisonous. As constrictors, they squeeze the life out of their prey. This snake's many pit organs are clearly visible.

Rattlesnake coiled for attack

Let's THINK like the Chachamim!

Who decided that snakes should hunt at night? Is it only a coincidence that mice and other creatures are more active in the dark? How did the viper get those pit organs to help it catch its meal? Where did this miraculous design come from and how does it know to only activate itself at temperatures similar to the prey's body? You know the answer — it could only be the doing of the *Borei Olam*!

SET YOUR SIGHTS ON SOME ANIMALS WITH A DIFFERENT POINT OF VIEW.

THERMAL IMAGING

Other Amazing Types of VISION

The Mantis Shrimp

This colorful shrimp has what is considered by biologists to be the most complex and sophisticated vision ever discovered. Each eye is bean-shaped and placed at the end of a stalk, making the eyes very flexible and elastic. The eyes move independently so one eye can be looking forward and the other backward at the same time. Each eye is divided into three sections — an upper section, a lower section and a band of super-special ommatidia (mini-eyes) running across the middle. This lets the shrimp see three separate images from its three sections all at the same time, and it gives the shrimp incredible 3D vision and depth perception from each of its eyes. If that were not enough, Hashem also gifted the mantis shrimp with the ability to see ultraviolet light and polarised light. These are "invisible" types of light that our eyes can't see. And there's more — the shrimp can decide which type of light to tune in to; this enables it to see things that might be invisible in normal light. Why was it given this ability? Because many of its prey are transparent and cannot be seen, so the mantis shrimp tunes in to a different type of vision to check whether its "invisible" prey is swimming or floating past.

The "All-Eye" Brittle Star

In the seas off Bermuda lives a very special starfish. Its official name is Ophiocoma wendtii and it's about the size of your hand. This starfish has a round disc-shaped body (like a large coin) with lots of thin long arms, and it can move incredibly fast. Ophiocoma is very special because the entire surface of its arms and body is covered with tiny, hard crystals. That's why it's called a brittle star. Scientists have recently discovered that these crystals are actually sophisticated lenses just like in a camera or in your own eye. Every single one of these tiny lenses (of which there are thousands covering the starfish) is plugged into a tiny nerve that senses the light passing through the crystal lens. This turns the entire starfish into one massive "all-seeing" eye. Could you imagine seeing with your toes and your chin as well?

The mantis shrimp

Brittlestar skin is entirely covered with crystal "eyes" that look similar to compound eyes of a fly.

I'M NOT SCARED OF YOU – I'M A MAN, NOT A MOUSE.

FUN FACT!

Scientists at the University of Michigan have developed a contact lens that can act as a night vision device. The lens has a thin strip of a substance called graphene that sits between layers of glass. It reacts to tiny amounts of light to make dark images look brighter.

Some animals have eyes superior to humans, to better see this world. But only humans have a *neshamah*, so they can see the Next World.

Rav Yisrael Greenwald *shlita*

JET ENGINE CONES

We know that airplanes fly because of the shape of their wings, but it's the engines hanging underneath that push the plane forward through the air. When we fly overseas, we're often traveling at almost 600 mph (over 1000 km/h). ▶

How do airplane ENGINE CONES work?

A jet engine is really a very advanced kind of table fan.

Imagine a little table fan that you use to cool yourself on a hot day. Its blades are slightly angled and are turning fast enough to suck the air in at the back of the fan and force it out at the front of the fan where you sit and enjoy the breeze. Jet engines are really just a whole set of massive fans that are arranged one behind the other. The largest fan sucks the air in front of the plane and forces it out behind the plane, pushing the plane forward. Other smaller fans in the middle of the engine suck some of the air into a chamber, compressing the air until it's under very high pressure. Fuel is mixed and burned in this air, which causes an explosion. The hot exhaust gas is forced out of the back of the engine like a rocket, also helping push the plane forward.

When engineers first designed fan and propeller engines for planes, they found that as the planes went faster they would reach a speed where the engines started choking (the engines would stall and stop). This happened because at very high speeds the air right in front of the fan blades or propeller began damming up, with most of it racing around the sides of the engine instead of going into and through the engine (which is where it needs to go!). They discovered that by putting a cone in the center of the fan or propeller, the wall of still air disappeared even at very high speeds. The cone acted to guide all the air directly in front of the fan and into the engine, rather than letting it build up like a wall.

Fan · High-pressure compressor · High-pressure shaft · Low-pressure shaft · Combustion chamber · Low-pressure compressor

Air flows around the wings, but at that speed the air hitting the engines weighs as much as nine double-decker buses! So what stops the air from damming up at the front of the engine?

Note the jet cone in the center of the engine.

The wind pressure in front of an airplane's engines is the same weight as nine double-decker buses!

Did Hashem already give us **clues to the PROPELLER CONE** in one of his creatures?

High-pressure turbine
Jet engine cutaway showing how a jet engine works
Low-pressure turbine
Nozzle

BEING FAST CAN BE AS PLAIN AS THE NOSE ON YOUR FACE...

67

JET ENGINE CONES

The PEREGRINE FALCON's strange nose

The peregrine falcon is not only the world's fastest bird, it's the fastest member of the entire animal kingdom. It hunts and eats mainly other birds, such as pigeons and doves, which it catches in mid-flight. First it soars up to a very high height, then it scans the sky below for prey. When it spots a bird flying way below, it "locks onto" its target like a missile, folds its wings into a specific shape and nosedives towards the ground. In this dive, it often reaches a speed of over 200 mph (320 km/hr). The highest measured speed of a peregrine falcon is an incredible 242 mph (389 km/h). At these speeds, it would be almost impossible for most living creatures to take a breath, and the wall of air pressure forcing itself into the nose and lungs would cause choking and tissue damage. Since everything about the peregrine falcon's body was designed by Hashem for catching prey at high speed, Hashem also placed a solid yellow "jet cone" directly in the middle of its nostrils! Just like a fighter jet, this nose cone directs the right amount of air into the nostrils during a dive, allowing the peregrine falcon to breathe.

Peregrine falcon nose cone is seen as a yellow cone in the centre of its nostrils.

These poor birds

Owl? 50 mph

Osprey? 50 mph

Egyptian Vulture? 60 mph

Peregrine Falcon! 242 mph

The peregrine falcon dives

Let's THINK like the Chachamim!

There are over 500 different birds of prey in the world. Eagles, vultures, owls and ospreys, to name a few. But Hashem put a nose cone only in the center of the peregrine falcon's nostril. That's because no other bird ambushes their prey at such high speeds like the peregrine falcon does. So no other bird needs the same protection!

A peregrine falcon just after catching a dove in mid-flight

THE SPORT OF FALCONRY WAS PRACTICED AS FAR BACK AS NINEVEH AND BAVEL.

...have **NO** nose cone...

Bald Eagle? 100 mph

Golden Eagle? 180 mph

וְקַל כַּנֶּשֶׁר...
לַעֲשׂוֹת רְצוֹן אָבִיךָ
שֶׁבַּשָּׁמַיִם

Be light as an eagle... to do the will of Your Father in Heaven.

Avos 5:20

ALL-WEATHER CLOTHING

Many people enjoy hiking. It's healthy, provides new energy to serve Hashem better and gives one a chance to marvel at His forests, mountains, lakes and landscapes. But what happens when a hiker is far from home and he's caught in the rain, wind or snow?

The technology of ALL-WEATHER CLOTHING

Have you ever been walking to shul on Shabbos and found yourself in a sudden downpour? It's not fun to arrive at your destination soaked to your skin. Neither your suit, pants or tzitzis are waterproof, so you have to wait for your body heat to dry off your clothing. In the meantime, you feel cold, uncomfortable and itchy. Even if you had worn a waterproof raincoat, you might be dry on the outside, but still wet on the inside. This is because you ran to shul to get out of the rain, sweating while doing so; the raincoat doesn't "breathe," so you get soaked from the inside from your sweat. Our clothing works well in normal weather conditions, but it is a challenge to design clothing that protects properly in extreme weather.

Thankfully we have scientists today that study and develop different fabrics to do different jobs, and sometimes they stick or "sandwich" them together to produce amazing results. Since hiking outdoors has become popular, these fabric "sandwiches" are used for pants and jackets and made to do the seeming impossible: they stop water getting *in* from the outside, yet they let trapped body heat and water (sweat) get *out* from the inside — all at the same time! This means that they are waterproof to keep you dry from the rain and snow, but at the same time they whisk away heat and sweat from your skin to keep you dry. The fabric sucks moisture off your skin and transports it to the outside of the fabric to let your skin breathe. Scientists often describe this fabric sandwich as being "directional." The inside layer of the fabric is dense and its fibers are hydrophilic (water is attracted to the fibers). Body moisture is immediately pulled away from the skin along the fibers to a more loosely-packed outer fiber where it can evaporate. On top of this, the outer layer of the fabric sandwich is treated with a special coating that is hydrophobic (this means it doesn't like water). Rain or snow that lands on the material from the outside is repelled and rolls away.

ALL-WEATHER CLOTHING

MAMMAL FUR — keeping dry in the wet

Fabric scientists looked to Hashem's creatures to solve the "no water in — body sweat out" problem. Mammals like bears, otters and seals all live in places that have cold or extremely wet weather, or spend most of their lives in water. The scientists studied their fur coats and discovered the following: each hair follicle in their skin grows one or two long, large, thick hairs called "guard hairs" that form the overcoat, and each follicle also grows a whole bunch of smaller, shorter and very fine hairs, called the undercoat. Amazingly, the dense undercoat actively pushes water, vapor and excess heat away from the skin, keeping them dry, while the natural oils that cover the overcoat hairs repel water and make it run off the fur, protecting the animal from getting soaked in a downpour. Although the animals are wet on the outside of their fur, against their skin they remain dry and comfortable.

The Polar Bear

Weighing in at up to 1500 lb (700 kg), snow-white **polar bears** live their entire lives at the edge of the pack-ice and in the sea around the Arctic Circle. The temperature is so cold there that they need both a fur coat and fat under their skins to insulate them. They have a 4 in (10 cm) layer of fat under their skins, plus an undercoat and overcoat similar to the sea otter. They are so well protected against the cold that they begin to overheat in temperatures over 50° F (10° C). They hunt seals and rarely eat anything other than the skin and blubber, which give them the most energy. Polar bears are excellent swimmers. One bear was tracked in 2011 and swam continuously for 9 days in the frigid Bering Sea for an incredible 400 mi (687 km) to reach pack-ice far from land.

The Sea Otter

Often found off the coast of Alaska, the **sea otter** lives in groups called "rafts" of between 10 and 1000 otters. They sleep floating on their backs; to stop themselves drifting apart, each otter holds the hands of another. The sea otter can literally live its entire life in the sea, never coming onto land. Its fur is the densest of any animal on earth; its skin has an estimated one million hairs per square inch. It needs this thick coat because, unlike sea mammals like whales and dolphins, it has no blubber to keep it warm. The dense undercoat and oil-covered overcoat work together to trap air close to the skin so the otter always remains warm and dry, even while swimming in the freezing sea.

A raft of sea otters holding hands to prevent them from drifting away from each other while sleeping

AUTONOMOUS CARS

Across the US, almost 3.5 million cars are damaged every year. Drivers not paying attention while driving often bump into the car in front of them, side-swipe another car while changing lanes, or end up running off the road. Now engineers are developing a technology that could prevent all these collisions from happening.

Collision avoidance technology senses the presence of other objects approaching the car.

Autonomous Car
Remote Sensing System

Diagram of the many technologies that need to work together to make an autonomous car drive safely

Driver, take your hands off the wheel

The race is on around the world to develop the first cars to be sold in showrooms that drive entirely by themselves. The most advanced versions of these cars won't even have steering wheels! They are called autonomous cars because they can sense their surroundings and both navigate and drive without human input. Many prototypes already exist and navigate our roads successfully. The technology used inside these cars is vast and extremely complicated. The car needs to have software to manage all the parts of the vehicle (acceleration, braking, turning corners, indicating, parking) and advanced optical and spatial technology — devices like multiple all-weather cameras, Lidar (a type of radar using laser beams), GPS, and IMU (a device that mimics the inner ear and measures the car's position in space, its acceleration and its angle with the road).

Combined together, these fantastic technologies will allow all these cars to drive humans around safely. The biggest concern, and the technology that's taking the longest to perfect, is a collision avoidance system. Why? Because currently most cars are still driven by people and unfortunately human error such as tiredness or distractions causes many accidents and collisions. Software scientists now have the challenge of developing computer programs that can instantly and smoothly link and process all the information being received by the technologies mentioned above, and then make split-second decisions on how to avoid a collision. It sounds easy, but it's extremely difficult to "train" a car to recognize the difference between an oncoming car traveling past normally and another one veering into its lane at the last second, between a pedestrian and a road sign, or a ball bouncing into the road and thick smoke. The autonomous car has to know what it can and should swerve away from, and what it should drive through.

Software engineers in Europe are studying a **very special insect** to help them design **COLLISION AVOIDANCE SOFTWARE.** Can you guess which one?

DON'T LET THE WAIT **PLAGUE** YOU; TURN THE PAGE!

AUTONOMOUS CARS

LOCUSTS really know how to drive! A while ago, a group of scientists took a closer look at swarms of locusts. They noticed something strange: These swarms are often made up of no less than 200 million locusts per square mile (80 million locusts per square kilometer), and yet despite all these millions of locusts taking off, landing and flying in different directions all at the same time, they never seem to crash into each other. The scientists wondered what properties these insects have that could help them build collision avoidance software for cars. They found it in the link between their eyes and their brains.

All eyes work in much the same way. Light from the world around us enters the eye and forms an image there. This image of light stimulates nerve fibers at the back of the eye. The nerves aren't long enough to reach the brain, so they form chains, sending an electrical signal that runs along the nerve, then jumps from the end of one nerve to the start of the next nerve, up the nerve chain to the brain where the image is read and understood. Vision is really amazing and we have much to be grateful for, but if locusts could talk, they'd have even more for which to thank Hashem. He has designed and given them a lobula giant movement detector, or LGMD for short. Simply put, this is a bundle of nerves that are different from the other nerves around them. They also form part of

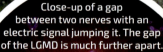

Close-up of a gap between two nerves with an electric signal jumping it. The gap of the LGMD is much further apart.

Locust swarm eating plants.

Let's THINK like the Chachamim!

A scientist studies this design in locusts and makes use of it for collision avoidance software. A chacham studies this design and sees the miraculous works of Hashem. Other non-swarming insects don't have a giant movement detector because they don't need one. Hashem places His technology and all the talents a creature requires exactly where they need to be. Our jobs are to keep developing our "Hashem detector" — it's called emunah.

the nerve chain to the locust's brain, but the gap where they link to the nerves coming from the eye (where they wait to catch the electrical signal) is much bigger. Most of the electrical signals are too small to jump the gap to the giant movement detector, so they just fizzle out. This means that most of the time, the LGMD nerves are having a nap! Billions of electrical signals in their fellow nerve chains around them are traveling up from the eye to the brain all the time, allowing the locust to see the world around them. And the LGMD remains asleep!

The locust we are studying is flying in a swarm and sees thousands of others flying around him, over him, under him, next to him, overtaking him, zooming diagonally across his path. He sees it all, his brain ignores it all, and he merrily keeps

his trajectory. But then something dangerous happens — another locust is flying directly towards our locust. The image of this locust "road hog" repeats itself over and over, getting bigger and bigger as it gets closer. The electrical signals build-up at the gap where the LGMD is sleeping until they become one giant signal that is big enough to jump the gap and wake up the LGMD. When that happens, an instantaneous signal is sent up the LGMD to very specific parts of the brain. In microseconds, action is taken and our locust adjusts his flight path to avoid the collision.

SOME LOCUSTS ARE KOSHER...BUT I THINK I'LL STICK TO STEAKS.

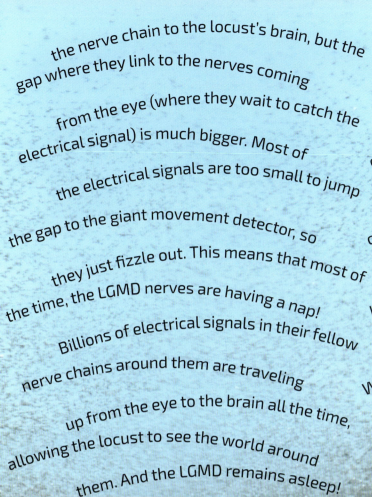

A nerve with its tangle of arms. The yellow dots show where an electrical signal is jumping from one nerve to another.

EVEN MORE **CRITTERS** WHO CAN DEFEND THEMSELVES!

AUTONOMOUS CARS

Creatures with Great SELF-DEFENSE

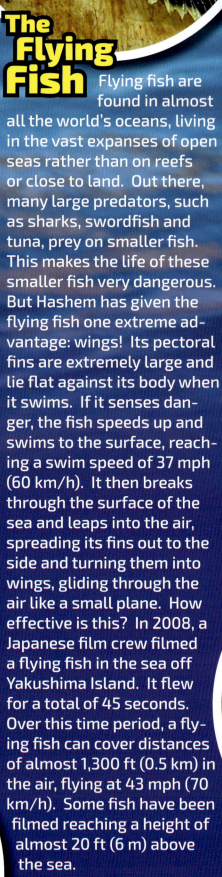

The Flying Fish

Flying fish are found in almost all the world's oceans, living in the vast expanses of open seas rather than on reefs or close to land. Out there, many large predators, such as sharks, swordfish and tuna, prey on smaller fish. This makes the life of these smaller fish very dangerous. But Hashem has given the flying fish one extreme advantage: wings! Its pectoral fins are extremely large and lie flat against its body when it swims. If it senses danger, the fish speeds up and swims to the surface, reaching a swim speed of 37 mph (60 km/h). It then breaks through the surface of the sea and leaps into the air, spreading its fins out to the side and turning them into wings, gliding through the air like a small plane. How effective is this? In 2008, a Japanese film crew filmed a flying fish in the sea off Yakushima Island. It flew for a total of 45 seconds. Over this time period, a flying fish can cover distances of almost 1,300 ft (0.5 km) in the air, flying at 43 mph (70 km/h). Some fish have been filmed reaching a height of almost 20 ft (6 m) above the sea.

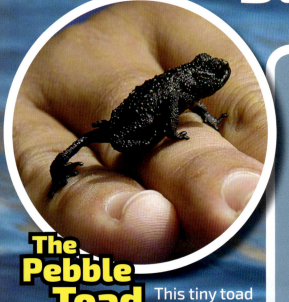

The Pangolin

The pangolin is the world's only mammal that is born with plate-like scales covering its body, rather than hair. These hard scales look like giant interlocking fingernails and have sharp edges. The pangolin is a docile creature and, like the anteater, uses its long sticky tongue to collect termites to eat. When it feels threatened, it rolls itself into a ball and covers its nose with its tail, turning itself into a ball of armor, like a giant pine cone that's hard and tough to break. When the threat has passed, the pangolin stretches out, retracting its scales like a rolling garage door, and goes on its merry way.

The Pebble Toad

This tiny toad measures only 0.8 in (2 cm) and lives in the high mountains of Venezuela in South America. It has a black rubbery skin and is extremely light, but it can't hop well like other frogs and toads — it's built for climbing. Up in these mountains its main predator is the tarantula, which is a large hairy spider that waits to ambush the toad as it climbs up the bare rock face looking for puddles and food. But the pebble toad has been gifted by Hashem with a trick up its sleeve. If ambushed, the toad pulls in its legs, tenses its muscles and turns into a round rubbery pebble, rolling and bouncing down the mountain to escape the tarantula. Because it's so light and its skin is so rubbery, it comes to no harm.

The Pom-Pom Crab

This cute little crab measures only 1 in (2.5 cm) and lives among the world's coral reefs. For defense, it resorts to two methods: it is brightly colored, as a warning to would-be predators to keep away; and it allows a toxic, stinging anemone to grow on each of its two front pincers. These two sea anemones live permanently on the crab's pincers; when the crab feels threatened, it waves the anemones around in front of itself like two pom-poms. The advantage to the crab? If a predator gets too close, it gets a poisonous sting from the anemones. The advantage to the anemones? They sit right on the pincers where the crab grasps its food. Any small particles of food wafting around the crab are conveniently eaten by the anemones.

HURRAH FOR THE POM-POM CRAB!

מֶלֶךְ אֵין לָאַרְבֶּה
וַיֵּצֵא חֹצֵץ כֻּלּוֹ

There is no king of the locusts, yet they all go out together.

Mishlei 30:27

COMPOSITES

Once upon a time, all airplanes and cars and even some boat parts were made with molded panels of metal joined together. Metals are heavy, and they rust and crack. How could engineers make things lighter and last longer? With hexagonal composites!

How do HEXAGONAL COMPOSITE PANELS work?

Most people would think that something solid, without any holes in it, is stronger than something that has holes in it. Believe it or not, that isn't true. One easy example of this is your own bones. If they were made of solid bone all the way through, you'd be many pounds heavier; you would find it more difficult to move, and it would be easier for you to break a bone. As strange as it sounds, your bones are hollow in the middle where the marrow is, and this makes them much stronger, not weaker. Engineers know this trick too: it's easier to bend a solid metal pole than a hollow metal pole. And hollow objects are lighter too, enabling them to move more easily.

Now think about the sheets or panels that cars, planes and boats are made of. How thick do you think they are? Believe it or not, between 2 mm and 4 mm thick — that's it! These panels make up the "skin" of the vehicle and are made to be extremely strong, to resist cracking, and yet be flexible at the same time. Engineers have found that the best materials for this are carbon composites. Composites are mixtures of man-made fibers that are mixed together for extra strength. But it's expensive stuff! So engineers had to figure out how to use the smallest amount of it to get the strongest, lightest panel (they call this an excellent strength-to-weight ratio). When they found how to do this, the panels made the vehicles lighter, stronger, and helped save fuel costs too...

...Can you guess what shape they use?

When this composite material is molded into the shape of hexagons that are laid in neat rows, the result is a flat panel that is extremely lightweight, extremely strong and uses the least amount of expensive composite.

Close-up of Kevlar composite made of hollow hexagons

Airplane construction, with thin composite panels for the airplane skin shown in the foreground

Sailing yacht hulls are made of hexagon composites.

It isn't too difficult to figure out where engineers looked in Hashem's world to find **THE BEST DESIGN.**

BUT HASHEM KNEW WHICH SHAPE WOULD **"BEE"** MOST EFFICIENT!

COMPOSITES

The honey we scoop from our jars comes from inside the honeycomb composite the bees make to store their honey.

HONEYCOMB — Hashem's brilliant composite

The structure of beehives and the sweet, liquid gold inside it has intrigued man for thousands of years. Bees live in colonies of thousands of individuals, all working in perfect unity for a common goal. Bees have eight wax-producing glands on their abdomens; the wax is shed in the form of small scales all the time. Some worker bees spend their time deep inside the hive, collecting the wax scales that have been dropped by the bees in the colony. They press and mold the wax scales together, forming empty hexagonal cylinders (called cells) that are fused into row upon row until the result is a honeycomb. Inside the empty honeycomb, bees either store their growing grubs, or make and store their food supply, which we all know as honey.

The bees could make any shape they wanted — the honeycomb could be made of rows of round cells or square cells or triangular cells. But Hashem imprints a specific design into the nature of bees, and they only make honeycomb cells hexagonal in shape. Guess what? Science, engineering and mathematics have shown clearly that the most efficient and strongest design for packing and storage is the hexagon. Absolutely no space is wasted, the most storage is created, it has the strongest walls and uses the least amount of wax. When the cells are empty, the honeycomb is the lightest it could be.

The transparent wax scales that bees make from their glands can be seen next to a match head and below a bee's wing.

IN 2014, A TWO-STORY BEEHIVE WITH 500,000 BEES WAS FOUND IN TEXAS.

Mind your own BEESWAX!

Did you know that beeswax is used in cosmetics, like lip balm, eye shadow and hand cream? It's also used for making candles, in shoe polish, as bone-wax (pressed onto bones during surgery to prevent bleeding), in chewing gum, and as a food-glazing agent to seal in freshness in fruits and cheeses. In ancient times, it was even used as fillings for tooth cavities!

Beeswax candles

Honey bee

Let's THINK like the Chachamim!

Why would bees have glands that automatically make scales of wax which flake off and lie around in their hives? Why would certain bees know to squish the scales together to make wax? How could it be that an insect with a brain no bigger than a pin-head could have the engineering skill to make perfect hexagonal cylinders? How do thousands of them work together to flawlessly make perfect honeycombs, the world's most efficient, strongest and lightest storage structure? All these talents are gifts from the *Borei Olam!*

HOW DID THESE CREATURES BUILD THEIR COMPOSITE SKILLS?

COMPOSITES

A World of Hashem's COMPOSITES

Malleefowl nest structure

egg chamber
sand insulation
rotting compost
earth

A malleefowl atop its mound

The Malleefowl

This strange bird from Australia is the size of a large chicken and has a talent for creating composites to ensure the perfect environment in which to incubate its eggs. Instead of building a nest and sitting on the eggs, the father malleefowl spends all his time building a massive incubator. He starts by scraping a hole in the earth about 3 ft (1 m) deep and 10 ft (3 m) wide. He then collects a composite of wood, leaves and sand and fills the hole until he has a heap almost 3 ft (1 m) above the ground. Then he waits for it to rain. Once the heap is wet, the vegetation begins to rot and create heat. The malleefowl spends its time turning and mixing the material until the temperature is just right. He then digs deep into it like an excavator and makes an egg cavity in which the mother lays her eggs. The eggs are incubated by the heat of the rotting composite; the male malleefowl spends his time poking his head into the heap, checking the temperature, and either digging holes into the top to let it cool a little or adding more moist litter to create more heat.

The
PAPER WASP
building its nest

The Paper Wasp

The paper wasp has its own unique composite with which to build its nests. It collects fibers from wood and plants, which it then chews up and mixes with saliva. The product is a whitish-gray pulp that it then slowly uses to build a hive that looks like a honeycomb made of paper rather than wax. It too knows the engineering secret of the hexagon, thanks to Hashem.

AND NOW FOR THE
"GLAND" FINALE...
FEATURING A CLIFFHANGER AND WEB BROWSER!

COMPOSITES

The Redback Spider (black widow)

Much feared for its venomous bite that could even kill a child, the redback spider has another talent that's just as awe-inspiring. It has a whopping 800 or more glands in its abdomen that manufacture up to six different varieties of silk. Spider silk is such a complex composite of different proteins and other substances, such as pyrrolidine and potassium nitrate, that all attempts to manufacture a synthetic (man-made) copy in large amounts have failed.

Why would we want to make a similar compound? Because Hashem has given spider silk the most amazing properties: compared by weight to other substances, a strand of spider silk is over five times stronger than high-grade alloy steel, up to ten times tougher than Kevlar (the composite used to make bullet-proof vests), and yet can stretch up to five times its relaxed length without breaking.

Spider silk is tougher than a bullet-proof vest.

The Edible-Nest Swiftlet

This small, sleek and fast little bird is a member of the swift family. It lives near the sea, where there's not much around to help build its nest. And since there are few trees available, it has to make its nest on the vertical cliff faces and in the sea caves of its surroundings. So what unique building material does Hashem supply it with? Unbelievably, it uses its own spit! The swiftlet has two large salivary glands that it uses to produce copious amounts of a sticky composite, made mainly of water and a nutrient-rich mix of proteins called mucin. The mucin dries rapidly and the swiftlet builds layer upon layer of this substance, eventually making a perfect, cup-shaped nest of dried saliva in which it lays its eggs. These nests are harvested by people and are used to make a soup called "bird's nest soup," which is a delicacy in the Far East. So prized is this soup that these bird nests are sold for up to $1,000 per pound (about half a kilogram). That's pretty expensive spit!

Swiftlet nests are used in traditional Asian cooking.

Swiftlet at its nest

The redback spider is also unique in that it doesn't spin a normal web; it lays out a massive and very messy 3-D web, seemingly an untidy tangle of different types of silk strands. Biologists have shown however, that this 3-D tangle is actually a precise structure of strands that are "spring-loaded" and allow the redback to pull its prey up to the top of its web, even when the prey is ten times the size and weight of the spider!

And speaking of amazing, its venom is another composite of liquid proteins, which causes death in its prey within minutes, and in humans causes a sickness called lactrodectism that may last more than 24 hours. It starts with severe pain around the bite site as well as nausea, vomiting, headache and agitation. In 1956 at the Commonwealth Serum Laboratories in Australia, Dr. Saul Wiener (after whom this book edition is named) developed the world's first antivenom to fight the bite of redback and black widow spiders. *Baruch Hashem*, it is still used today. In Australia alone it's estimated that between 2,000 and 10,000 redback spider bites occur every year.

A spider's spinnerets spinning the silk as it exits the silk glands

The tangled web of a redback spider is a masterful trap that can even catch much larger animals, like a lizard.

Dr Saul Wiener, inventor of the redback spider antivenom

THEN ALONG CAME DR. WIENER AND STOPPED THAT OLD SPIDER...

כִּדְבוֹרִים הָיוּ בָּנַי, מִתְנַהֲגִים בָּעוֹלָם עַל יְדֵי צַדִּיקִים

My children are like bees, who are led through life by tzaddikim [as the Queen Bee leads the hive].

Devarim Rabbah 1:6

Image Credits

Title Page: Wikimedia Commons – Shuttle launch, courtesy: NASA

Guns, pp. 8–9: Shutterstock; Wikimedia Commons – Blank bullet, courtesy: Sylt90

Guns, pp. 10–11: Shutterstock; Wikimedia Commons – Pistol shrimp, courtesy: Arthur Anker

Rockets, pp. 12–13: Shutterstock; Wikimedia Commons – Stamp, courtesy: US Bureau of Engraving and Printing / Rocket diagram, courtesy: Code.pump / Astronaut on the moon, courtesy: NASA / Saturn V rocket, courtesy: NASA

Rockets, pp. 14–15: Wikimedia Commons – Supply rocket exploding, courtesy: NASA, Joel Kowsky / Challenger explosion, courtesy: Kennedy Space Centre / Challenger before explosion, courtesy: NASA / Bombadier beetle, courtesy: cc-by-sa-2.5; US Launch Report – SpaceX explosion

Rockets, pp. 16–17: Shutterstock; Reinhard Weidlich – Ant attacks bombadier beetle; Minden Pictures – Bombadier spraying, courtesy: Satoshi Kuribayashi; Wikimedia Commons – Bombadier beetle, courtesy: Dave Hill

GPS, pp. 18–19: Shutterstock; Wikimedia Commons – Roger Easton, courtesy: National Inventors Hall of Fame / Butterfly jewel, courtesy: Adam Alexandru / Navstar-2F, courtesy: USAF / GPS satellite network, courtesy: NOAA; Flikr – Using GPS in car, courtesy: daveiam; Mykolastock – Globe

GPS, pp. 20–21: Shutterstock; Wikimedia Commons – Monarch caterpillar, courtesy: Antilived / Milkweed flowers, courtesy: David Whelan / Monarch chrysalis, courtesy: CSIRO / Monarch emerging, courtesy: aussiegall

Tasers, pp. 22–23: Shutterstock; Wikimedia Commons – Taser X-26, courtesy: junglecat / Barbed Taser dart, courtesy: US Military

Tasers, pp. 24–25: Shutterstock; Wikimedia Commons – Amazon River, courtesy: Jason Hollinger / US power socket, courtesy: Legoktm / Electric eel muscle fibers, courtesy: National Institute of Standards and Technology / Electric eel, courtesy: opencage; Flikr – Electric eel sensory pits, courtesy: ravas51

Camouflage, pp. 26–27: Shutterstock; Wikimedia Commons – Cell phone tower, courtesy: Gary Minnaert / Soldier camouflaging face, courtesy: SPC Gerald James

Camouflage, pp. 28–29: Shutterstock; Wikimedia Commons – Banded sea snake, courtesy: Nhobgood / Mimic octopus, courtesy: Steve Childs / Coral crab, courtesy: Tanaka Juuyoh / Mimic Octopus, courtesy: Laika ac / Mimic octopus, courtesy: Silke Baron

Camouflage, pp. 30–31: Shutterstock; Wikimedia Commons – Ant, courtesy: William Cho / Ant spider, courtesy: Charles Lam / Owl butterfly, courtesy: gbohne / Owl, courtesy: Superior National Forest

Antifreeze, pp. 32–33: Shutterstock; Wikimedia Commons – Antifreeze in engine, courtesy: Evelyn Giggles

Antifreeze, pp. 34–35: Shutterstock; Wikimedia Commons – Wood frog thawing, courtesy: Emilyk; Flikr – Frozen wood frog, courtesy: Jay Cross / Wood frog, courtesy: Brian Gratwicke

Antifreeze, pp. 36–37: Shutterstock; Wikimedia Commons – Surinam toad skin close-up, courtesy: Endeneon / Surinam toad specimen, courtesy: Emőke Dénes / Surinam toad, courtesy: Hugo Claessen / Turtle frog, courtesy: Paul J. Morris / Turtle frog, courtesy: Stephen Zozaya; Flikr – Harlequin poison dart frog, courtesy: Sebastian Moreno / Strawberry poison dart frog, courtesy: Pavel Kirillov / Wallace's flying frog, courtesy: Rushen; Minden Pictures – Flying frog, courtesy: Steven Dalton

Antifreeze, pp.38–39: Shutterstock; Wikimedia Commons – Glass frog, courtesy: JurriaanH / Glass frog underside, courtesy: Geoff Gallice; Flikr – Cocoon frog, courtesy: Tnarg 12345; Creative Commons – Gastric brooding frog diagram, courtesy: Guerrero, Anna; Science Source Imaging – Gastric brooding frog, courtesy: Michael J Tyler

Sports Cars, pp. 40–41: Shutterstock; Wikimedia Commons – Carl Benz, Public Domain / 1885 Benz Car, Public Domain

Sports Cars, pp. 42–43: Shutterstock; Wikimedia Commons – Peel P50, courtesy: Vauxford / American Dream, courtesy: Vetatur Fumare; Flikr – Ferrari 250 GTO, courtesy: Roderick Eime / Bugatti Veyron Super Sport, courtesy: Shane K

Sports Cars, pp. 44–45: Shutterstock; Wikimedia Commons – Cheetah tail, courtesy: Deepanshu Ahlawat / Cheetah head profile, courtesy: Tony Hisgett / Cheetah nails, courtesy: David J. Stang / Cheetah chest diagram, courtesy: Coluberssymbol

Sports Cars, pp. 46–47: Shutterstock; Wikimedia Commons – Banana slugs on hand, courtesy: Ralph Arvesen / Banana slugs, courtesy: Andy.goryachev / Lichen on tree, courtesy: Lynn Greyling / Lichen on stone, courtesy: Roantrum / Mite, courtesy: S.E. Thorpe / Peregrine falcon, courtesy: Mike Baird / Three-toed sloth, courtesy: Tauchgurke / Sloth skeleton, courtesy: Joxerra Aihartza / Peregrine falcon eating pigeon, courtesy: Geo Swan / Douglas D-558-2 Skyrocket, courtesy: US Navy / Khalid-Bin-Mohsen-Shaari, courtesy: FableMaker

Welding Helmets, pp. 48–49: Shutterstock; Wikimedia Commons – Man welding, courtesy: bniegel / Arc eyes, courtesy: Cdale0112 / Speedglas welding helmet, courtesy: Ergonomidesign / Photochromic lenses, courtesy: Vista Lowcost

Welding Helmets, pp. 50–51: Shutterstock

Welding Helmets, pp. 52–53: Shutterstock

Welding Helmets, pp. 54–55: Shutterstock; Wikimedia Commons – Diagram of cuttlefish cells, courtesy: Cuttlefish Optimization Algorithm / Cuttlefish, courtesy: Hans Hillewaert / Cuttlefish skin close-up, courtesy: Minette

Sunscreen, pp.56–57: Shutterstock; Wikimedia Commons – Red Vet Pet; Pixabay – Sunscreen bottle, courtesy: markusmarcinek

Sunscreen, pp. 58–59: Shutterstock; Wikimedia Commons – Hippo skull, courtesy: Raul654 / Hippo submerged, courtesy: Calle v H / Hipposudoric acid, courtesy: Evercat / Hippo mouth, courtesy: koles

Thermal Imaging, pp. 60–61: Shutterstock; Wikimedia Commons – Kalman Tihanyi, courtesy: nieznany / Night vision screen, courtesy: AlexPlank; Flikr – Night vision camera, courtesy: Program Executive Office Soldier

Thermal Imaging, pp. 62–63: Daniel Weiss Commercial Photography – Albino Burmese python; Shutterstock; Wikimedia Commons – Eyelash viper, courtesy: Geoff Gallice / Pit organ diagram, courtesy: Serpent nirvana

Thermal Imaging, pp. 64–65: Shutterstock; Wikimedia Commons – compound eye close-up, courtesy: Nation kingdom; Flikr – Mantis shrimp, courtesy: Charlene Mcbride

Jet Engine Cones, pp. 66–67: Shutterstock; Wikimedia Commons – Jet engine cutaway diagram, courtesy: K. Aainsqatsi

Jet Engine Cones, pp. 68–69: Shutterstock; Wikimedia Commons – Bald eagle, courtesy: Saffron Blaze / Egyptian vulture, courtesy: Carlos Delgado / Golden eagle, courtesy: Rizkuwait / Osprey, courtesy: Simon Carrasco / Peregrine falcon nose cone, courtesy: Greg Hume; Pexels – Owl, public domain.

All Weather Clothing, pp. 70–71: Shutterstock; Wikimedia Commons – Hydrophobic fabric, courtesy: Brocken Inaglory

All Weather Clothing, pp. 72–73: Shutterstock; Wikimedia Commons – Polar bear underwater, courtesy: Detroit Zoo, Roy Lewis / Sea otter, courtesy: Marshal Hedin / Sea otter raft, courtesy: Judy Gallagher / Inuit photo, Public Domain; British Antarctic Survey – Seal fur cross-section, courtesy: Pete Bucktrout

Autonomous Cars, pp. 74–75: Shutterstock

Autonomous Cars, pp. 76–77: Shutterstock; Flikr – Locust swarm, courtesy: Laika ac

Autonomous Cars, pp. 78–79: Shutterstock; Wikimedia Commons – Flying fish specimen, courtesy: Shannon Rankin NOAA / Pangolin curled up, courtesy: Manis temminckii; Flikr – Pom pom crab, courtesy: Rebecca Tse / Pebble toad, courtesy: guilherme jofili

Composites, pp. 80–81: Shutterstock; Wikimedia Commons – Airplane construction, courtesy: USAF Kelly White

Composites, pp. 82–83: Shutterstock; Wikimedia Commons – Honeybee close-up, courtesy: Makro Freak / Wax scales, courtesy: Waugsberg; Pixabay – Beeswax candles, courtesy: schnullibiene; Flikr – Beeswax lip balm, courtesy: Joanne Saige Lee

Composites, pp. 84–85: Shutterstock; Wikimedia Commons – Malleefowl, courtesy: butupa / Malleefowl nest, courtesy: Glen Fergus / Mallefowl nest structure diagram, courtesy: Pengo / Paperwasp, courtesy: Alvesgaspar

Composites, pp. 86–87: Shutterstock; Wikimedia Commons – Spinnerets spinning silk, courtesy: Jason7825 / Redback spider, courtesy: Marshal Hedin / Redback spider with lizard, courtesy: Calistemon / Bullet-proof vest, courtesy: US Army; Mrs Fay Wiener – Photo of Dr. Saul Wiener z"l